# Edward de Vere and the Shakespeare Printers

# Edward de Vere and the Shakespeare Printers

by Robert Sean Brazil

Published by Cortical Output, LLC, Seattle, WA USA

# CONTENTS

# About this Book

This second edition of *Edward de Vere and the Shakespeare Printers* features an improved text, more graphics, and attempts to offer as much information as possible in a format that can be comprehended by any reader, without prior knowledge of the Shakespeare controversies.

This version was essentially complete at the time of the author's death in 2010, lacking only some reference material. It has been thought best to present the material that is at hand, as it is.

# Acknowledgements

Thanks to my friends and family who have supported this endeavor, with encouragement and bemusement: The Right Reverend David Z. Brazil , The Right Honorable Dr. Percy Brazil , Jessie Brazil , Lisa Duff.

And many thanks to my far-flung fellow researchers and correspondents: Mick Clarke, Barboura Flues, Nina Green, Andy Hannas, Roger Stritmatter, and Dr. Jack Shuttleworth

Robert Sean Brazil, 2010

This edition of Edward de Vere and the Oxford Printers was produced by Tony Brazil, Lisa Duff, and Jefferson Foote.

# PART ONE :
## "Some enigma, some riddle"

ARMADO. *Some enigma, some riddle; come, thy l'envoy; begin.*

*Loves Labours Lost, III: 1*

# Chapter One

## The Shakespeare Problem

You may ask : what Shakespeare problem ?

He's been the most successful screenwriter of the 1990's and 2000's and he never has to be paid. He gets away with crude jokes that would be called tasteless anywhere else. Shakespeare's just fine the way he is! Shakespeare is High and Low. Shakespeare is gay and straight. The Bard, whose personal story is unknown and unquestioned, has been reduced to an Icon or symbol of rarefied intelligence, of impenetrable, unreachable genius. All things to all readers, the author has conveniently disappeared in favor of his words.

The problem has emerged because the few biographical facts that exist about  Mr. Shaksper of  Stratford-on-Avon don't tally with what we would expect from the brilliant author of the plays and poems. The content, attitude, life experience , interests, and deep classical education evident in the plays surpass what is on record for William Shaksper of Stratford-on-Avon.  Nothing in his life suggests that he was the author of the Shakespeare Canon, or had a reputation in his own lifetime to that effect.

The man commonly accepted to be the author  Shakespeare was born in the village of Stratford-on-Avon in April of 1564. There is no record of his actual birthday, but the boy was christened on April 26, 1564, and his name, as given was Gulielmus Shaksper.  No, he wasn't Italian, … "Gulielmus" was the Latin spelling of William. The Shaksper family's name is spelled dozens of different ways, but the most frequent, in his own time, was Shaksper, or Shaxper.  The boy's father, John Shaksper, was a glove maker. William Shaksper himself was essentially a grocer, grain trader and landlord by profession. No one in the village of Stratford thought of him as learned, bookish,  poetical or theatrical,

3

nor are there any legends, let alone records, of him producing any local entertainment. The local records only confirm that William Shaksper was a merchant, not a lyricist or genius of letters. Shaksper's will mentions no books or manuscripts. There is no remnant of any evidence that he was even literate himself. His parents and his children could not read. (What writer would not teach his own children to read?) Nor did his children benefit, or show they had any knowledge of his alleged celebrity as a playwright. The few historical connections that would place Shaksper as an actor or investor in the Globe Theater, or any other theatrical enterprise, were all created after the "fact". There is no contemporaneous evidence that Shaksper, the grain dealer of Stratford, was the author of the Shake-Speare Plays & Poems.

In short, there is a rather big Shakespeare Problem, and it is one of the greatest historical and literary mysteries of all time. The modern image of Shakespeare the Author , in his quaint country cottage, writing for a living while suing his neighbors in small claims court is a myth. The facts concerning William Shaksper of Stratford-on-Avon tell a different story.

# Chapter Two

# The Case Against Shaksper of Stratford in Brief:

*or*

## 33 Reasons to Doubt that Mr. Shaksper Wrote Shakespeare

1. There has never been found any authentic writing of any sort by William Shaksper of Stratford beyond six shaky signatures affixed to legal documents. Each of these differs from the others and they are all from the end phase of his life: 1612-1616. Three of these signatures are on his will, one is on a deposition in a breach-of-promise case, and two are on real-estate documents. None are related to plays, poetry, or publishing.

2. In his Last Will, no books , papers, or unpublished MSS are mentioned. He did not have a private library of any sort. No books have emerged that bear his signature, bookplate, or any other such identifier. His children inherited no books, not even a family Bible.

3. Shaksper's parents were illiterate. His daughters remained illiterate and unlearned. Judith Shaksper affixed a mark instead of a signature. The Shakespeare plays abound with female characters who read, who discuss philosophy, who are in every way literate. In a household in which erudition and wit would have erupted daily, how could Shakespeare's daughters not be influenced?

4. There is no record of education for Shaksper, either elementary or higher. His name does not appear in any College matriculation rolls. How he educated himself, if he did, is a mystery. The profound learning, and familiarity with French, Italian, Latin, and even Greek that emerges in the Shakespeare plays had to come from somewhere.

5. Nothing in contemporary Stratford-on-Avon history suggests he was a writer. The men of Stratford knew William Shaksper only as a grain dealer and property owner.

6. The link in Shaksper's will to Hemynge, Burbage, and Condell, is a visible interpolation, an after the fact addition.

7. This Shaksper's will contains nothing about shares in the Globe or Blackfriars theaters, and his heirs never received any payments, nor sought any.

8. All of the contemporary allusions to Shake-Speare the writer are enigmatic and in no way refer to the man in Stratford. The only things that indicate that this Stratford man was the dramatist are the posthumous vague assertions in the *First Folio* introductions and the peculiar inscriptions on the Stratford Monument.

9. There is nothing contemporary to the relevant time period that show that THIS Shaksper was connected with London theaters. There are but three or four references to a Will Shakespeare as an actor, and they are only in the period of 1598 to 1603. And several key instances have been misstated. Stratford defenders say that the Cast lists for Ben Jonson's *Every man in his Humour* 1598, show that Shakespeare acted in that play. But the cast list doesn't appear in the 1598 quarto, only in the 1616 *Collected Workes* of Jonson. The same is true for the *Sejanus* 1603 references; they date from 1616. There are two other recorded transactions that name a Shakespeare as involved financially in the King's men, and in capacity of receipt of cloth. In any case, there is no evidence that Shaksper of Stratford was an actor, or had a reputation as an actor on the London stages, or anywhere else. The few mentions of a Shakespeare

involved with the theater are in no way linked, until decades later, to the man from Stratford.

10. There were no eulogies to Shakespeare in 1616 when Shaksper died. His passing was a non-event, while Philip Sidney had been given a funeral of near Royal proportions.

11. Shaksper of Stratford was involved in numerous petty lawsuits, small claims court proceedings that indicate an attachment to money , however small, that is antithetical to the point of view of the Author of the plays and poems.

12. When Shaksper died in 1616, there were at least 16 masterpiece plays that had never been published. These plays appeared in print for the first time in the *Folio* of 1623. Many of these plays were not even performed in the era in which they were allegedly written. If Shaksper "wrote for money", why would Shaksper not exploit the potential market value of his "back catalog" ? If the rights to Shaksper's assets passed to his daughter Susanna, as residuary legatee, why did she never claim any books or manuscripts as a portion of the residuary estate?

13. When the Sonnets were published in 1609, Shaksper was alive. He took no action, he received no compensation. The introduction implies the author is dead. The naughty eroticism and personal revelations do not match Shaksper's lifestyle, and it is unlikely that a living author would permit his private diary of secret thoughts to be issued publicly.

14. Shaksper's rustic Warwickshire lifestyle is made fun of in the plays. There are only scant references to small farm animals, but numerous references to horses, cattle, hawks, and animals familiar to the nobility.

15. There is no indication that Shaksper left Stratford for London prior to 1585. His wife gave birth to twins that year, and while he may have left in a hurry, all evidence is that he had been "down on the farm" from 1564 to 1585. His sojourn in London after 1585 is mostly conjectural. But allusions and topical references in many of the Shakespeare plays clearly refer to Court intrigues in the 1576 to 1585 time period. There is no way Shaksper could have known about these matters first hand.

16. There are a number of Shakespeare-like "Apocryphal and Anonymous Plays", that are ruled out of the Shakespeare Canon, because they had a stage history or publication record that doesn't match the dates for Shaksper of Stratford. Some of the apocryphal plays are now being seen to be remarkably Shakespearean in language & plotting, but emerged too early for Shaksper to have written them.

17. Nothing in Shaksper's biography indicates sea voyages, knowledge of Italian manners, hawking, jousting, military service, legal training, foreign languages, and the Classics.

18. The Monument to Shakespeare in the Church at Stratford-on-Avon is not the original monument, which was sketched in the 17th century and shows a man with a sack, not a man writing on a pillow. The wording on the monument is extraordinarily peculiar, and can be shown to reveal that Shaksper was a front man for someone else.

19. "The retirement" of Shaksper, from London back to Stratford, is roughly coincidental with the name "William Shake-speare" appearing on plays, and the first notices that Shakespeare was the name of a writer of note. The standard "story" is that Shaksper "commuted" from Warwickshire to London to act in

plays, but this is infeasible and unsupported by any evidence.

20. All attempts at finding relevant material by tracing the Shaksper family have come up empty.

21. There is nothing to link Shaksper of Stratford to the Earl of Southampton, his alleged Patron. The dedications to Southampton in *Venus & Adonis* and *Lucrece* show that the author knew him well, and was on close familiar terms. Scholars have turned England upside down to find even a scrap of paper connecting Southampton to the man from Stratford. No such documents have been found.

22. Although there are plenty of pay-records for other actors of his day, there is no such data for Shaksper. The first notice that a "William Shakespeare" had been an actor comes from the printed quarto *Every Man in His Humour*, by Ben Jonson in 1598. The *Folio* of 1623, in part edited by Jonson, also lists "Shakespeare" as an actor in his plays. But the alleged links between the *Folio* Shakespeare and Shaksper of Stratford, are thin and frayed to the breaking point.

23. Court testimony from 1615 (the Ostler suit) includes the statement that the Shakespeare associated with the Globe Theater was dead, and could not testify. Shaksper was still alive in 1615.

24. It remains unknown where and how Shaksper got the money to buy his large house in Stratford. He certainly did not earn it through the theater or publishing.

25. No link is known between Shaksper and any of the known writers of his day, except possibly Ben Jonson who tells both sides of the story, by praising Shakes-speare (in the *Folio*) while slamming Shaksper, as

"Sogliardo", the country bumpkin who tries to buy a coat of arms in *Every Man Out of His Humor*.

26. Edward Alleyn, a famous Elizabethan actor and theater owner, noted in his diaries the names of all the actors and hired dramatists of his time, and the names of all persons who received money in connection with the production of plays at the Fortune, Blackfriars, and other theaters. Alleyn never even once mentions Shaksper.

27. Henslowe's theatrical diary never mentions Shaksper or Shakespeare, even though he names all of the other famous writers who worked for him at one time including Chapman, Day, Dekker, Drayton, Heywood, Jonson, Marston, Middleton, Munday, Webster and others. He does mention the names of some of the Plays we call Shakespeare's, but they are left anonymous. The conclusion is that Henslowe never paid a penny to anyone named Shaksper or Shakespeare, and that the source of the Shakespeare plays was rather different than Henslowe's standard stable of paid providers of entertainment.

28. Shakspere allegedly lived in London for more than twenty years. But there are no remembrances of him or anecdotes of encounters with him by the contemporary writers and diarists of the time. How could Shakespeare, the person, be unknown to the intelligentsia of his time? Shakespeare the author seems to have known the most intimate details of the private lives of England's aristocracy. If "Shake-speare" knew them, they must have known him, perhaps he was even one of them. Could the ruling class of London have known the Bard by another name?

29. William Camden's *Britannia*, 1610, contains several references to Stratford-on-Avon. But he makes no mention of Shakespeare or Shaksper. Camden

certainly knew about the Shakespeare plays, and had praised "Shakespeare" the writer, but in no way connects them or their author with Stratford-on-Avon. Camden's list of "Worthies" for Stratford in 1605 does not mention Shaksper, nor does his "Annals" for the year 1616. William Camden, a prodigious historian and antiquary, who knew everything and everyone in England, and had even signed off on Shaksper's application for a coat of arms, clearly didn't think that Shaksper was notable, and certainly did not connect him in any way with the writer named Shakespeare.

30. Michael Drayton's *Poly Olbion*, 1613, contains detailed maps and an epic poem of all the interesting places in England. His map of Warwickshire does not even include Stratford-on-Avon. Drayton, who hailed from Warwickshire himself, would have known and remembered Shaksper, if the man was Drayton's inspiration, Shakespeare.

31. During the English Civil War, an Army surgeon named James Cooke, who found himself stationed at Stratford-on-Avon in 1642, sought out Shakspere's daughter Susanna, who was at that time a widow and known as Mrs. Susanna Hall. He asked her to show him any manuscripts or books that might have belonged to her father. He noted with surprise and disappointment that she had no knowledge of any books or documents, relating to William Shaksper. The only written material was that of Dr. Hall. Susanna herself never learned to read or write. This hardly sounds like the daughter of the greatest reader and writer in history.

32. The Globe Theater burned to the ground on June 28, 1613, In a published account of the disastrous fire, reference is made to Richard Burbage, Henry Condell and other Globe officials but nothing is said about Shaksper.

33. Dr. John Hall was a prominent physician who married Susanna Shaksper in 1607. He was thus "Shakespeare's son-in-law". Dr. Hall logged every volume in his library, but there was no mention of Shakespeare books, manuscripts or memorabilia. As Susanna and Dr. Hall were the residuary legatees and executives of the estate of William Shaksper, it is incredible that there was not a scrap of material related to the alleged literary career of their dad. Dr. Hall kept a detailed log of patient histories and anecdotes but he never mentions William Shakespeare. Hall does note that he treated Michael Drayton, the other notable poet of the era from Warwickshire. "Mr. Drayton, an excellent poet, I cured him of a certain fever with syrup of violets'.

# Chapter Three

# The Authorship Investigation and Debate

Because of the peculiar facts stated above and more, critical doubt about the prevailing myth of the Shakespeare phenomenon has been raised over the past several centuries by some of the greatest minds in Literature, Philosophy, and Science:

Charles Dickens (1812-1870) "It is a great comfort, to my way of thinking, that so little is known concerning the poet. The life of Shakespeare is a fine mystery, and I tremble every day lest something should turn up."

Walt Whitman (1819-1892) "Conceived out of the fullest heat and pulse of European feudalism, personifying in unparalleled ways the medieval aristocracy, its towering spirit of ruthless and gigantic caste, its own peculiar air and arrogance (no mere imitation) one of the wolfish earls so plenteous in the plays themselves, or some born descendent and knower, might seem to be the true author of those amazing works... I am firm against Shaksper. I mean the Avon man, the actor."

Mark Twain (Samuel Clemens 1835-1910) "Shall I set down the rest of the Conjectures which constitute the giant Biography of William Shakespeare ? It would strain the Unabridged Dictionary to hold them. He is a Brontosaur: nine bones and six hundred barrels of plaster of paris ... Am I trying to convince anybody that Shakspere did not write Shakespeare's Works? Ah now, what do you take me for ?

Henry James (1843-1916) "I am... haunted by the conviction that the divine William is the biggest and most successful fraud ever practiced on a patient world."

Sigmund Freud (1856-1939) "I no longer believe that William Shakespeare, the actor from Stratford was the author of the

works which have so long been attributed to him. Since the publication of ... 'Shakespeare Identified', I am almost convinced that in fact Edward de Vere, Earl of Oxford is concealed behind this pseudonym "
< Footnote, by Freud, in the 1930 edition of *The Interpretation of Dreams* >

"We will have a lot to discuss about Shakespeare. I do not know what still attracts you to the man of Stratford. He seems to have nothing at all to justify his claim, whereas Oxford has almost everything. It is quite inconceivable to me that Shakespeare should have got everything secondhand – Hamlet's neurosis, Lear's madness, Macbeth's defiance and the character of Lady Macbeth, Othello's jealousy etc. It almost irritates me that you should support the notion."
<Letter from Freud to A. Zweig, 1937>

Charlie Chaplin (1889-1977) "In the work of the greatest geniuses, humble beginnings will reveal themselves somewhere but one cannot trace the slightest sign of them in Shakespeare... Whoever wrote [Shakespeare] had an aristocratic attitude."

Orson Welles (1915-85) "I think Oxford wrote Shakespeare. If you don't, there are some awfully funny coincidences to explain away."

Justice Harry A. Blackmun (1908-1999). "Oxfordians have come closer to proving their case than any other dissenters"

Justice John Paul Stevens (1920-) "First, where is Shakespeare's library? ... Second, his son-in-law's detailed medical journals ... make no mention of his illustrious father-in-law... finally, the seven year period of silence that followed Shakespeare's death in 1616 ... Perhaps he did not merit a crypt in Westminster Abbey, or a eulogy penned by King James, but it does seem odd that not even a cocker spaniel or a dachshund made any noise at all when he passed from the scene."

## The Search for the hidden Author

The earliest speculation about a hidden hand behind the Shakespeare plays was in 1785, when the Reverend James Wilmot, D.D. attributed the authorship to Sir Francis Bacon. In 1848, an American consulate named Joseph C. Hart speculated in his book, *The Romance of Yachting*, that the Stratford man could not have written the plays. Hart proposed Ben Jonson as the author.

The issue became popular knowledge in 1857 with the appearance of *The Philosophy of the Plays of Shakespeare Unfolded*, by Delia Bacon. Nathaniel Hawthorne wrote the preface, and helped with both the publication and promotion. This can be considered to be the first Anti-Stratfordian book. Although this work is ponderous, pretentious, and thin on facts, the author launched a whole genre of thought and criticism with her idea that the Shakespeare plays were a vehicle for a new philosophy, that looked beyond religious minutiae, and was based on a higher love and reason. Because of her name, (though she was not related to Francis Bacon), people have assumed that Delia Bacon was the first Baconian. She was not. Delia believed in a group theory of authorship, though she offered that Francis Bacon supplied the philosophy that infuses the plays. In her book, she named Sir Walter Raleigh as the mastermind who created the Shakespeare Plays, using the talents of a circle of men. In Delia's view this is how it went with Raleigh and Company:

"He became at once the centre of that little circle of high born wits and poets, the elder wits and poets of the Elizabethan age, that were then in their meridian there. Sir Philip Sidney, Thomas Lord Buckhurst, Henry Lord Paget, Edward Earl of Oxford, and some other, are included in the contemporary list of this courtly company, whose doings are somewhat mysteriously adverted to by a critic, who refers to the condition of the Art of Poesy at that time ."

Though most of Delia Bacon's "insights" were misguided, she did open the field to investigation, and she did name the man (Edward de Vere, the 17<sup>th</sup> Earl of Oxford) who has emerged, 140 + years after her lucky guess, as the strongest candidate for the authorship of the Shakespeare Canon.

## Problems with the Bacon Theory

After Delia Bacon's book, the floodgates of speculation opened and a torrent of research and nonsense was focused on the Shakespeare problem. A cult soon developed around a legend of a near-superhuman Francis Bacon, who was allegedly the brain behind everything renaissance and revolutionary in the 16<sup>th</sup> and 17<sup>th</sup> centuries. The reach was too far, the methodology was laughable faux-cryptography, and the result was universal ridicule.

In knocking down the case for Bacon, the biggest culprit is Francis himself. Bacon's voluminous other writings show none of the poetry, playfulness, or street level vulgarity associated with Shakespeare. Matching passages of aphorisms and the like are easily explained by the fact that Bacon was reading Shakespeare, and that sometimes both authors had read and made use of the same sources.

The many references to the "Boar" symbol in Shakespeare were latched onto by Baconians as referring to Bacon. In this instance they are close to the truth. They are right that the boar is symbolic of a person, but it is the Blue Boar, the badge of the Earls of Oxford..

In the World War I era, research into the authorship problem took a different turn. Robert Fraser's *The Silent Shakespeare*, 1915, offered William Stanley, the 6th Earl of Derby as the W.S. behind the Shakespeare name. In 1919 Abel Lefranc published *Sous le Masque de "William Shakespeare"*. LeFranc also zeroed in on William Stanley, who was the son-in-law of the 17<sup>th</sup> Earl of Oxford.

The watershed year in this field was 1920, when John Thomas Looney, a British schoolteacher proposed the theory that Edward de Vere, 17th Earl of Oxford, a Courtier to Queen Elizabeth I, was the author of the Shakespeare plays and poems. He outlined his hypothesis and discoveries in his book, *"Shakespeare" Identified*. This book had a wide reaching impact among intellectuals. It was reviewed favorably in the London press by John Galsworthy. Both Sigmund Freud and James Joyce read *"Shakespeare" Identified* and wrote about their impressions. Freud actually revised his interpretation of *Hamlet* in the light of his new understanding.

### Shakespearean Paradigms

The "Status Quo" opinion seems to be that "Shakespeare is just fine the way he is." This is essentially the **Stratfordian** Paradigm. Shakespeare is seen as a miraculous freak of nature: a self educated country merchant who somehow learned the theater inside and out and wrote the plays for money, and nothing more. Within the Stratfordian position there are a thousand mythical biographies of Shakespeare, based on each modern author's deconstruction of the plays and poems, with the few flimsy facts about Shaksper thrown in for color.

The next paradigm or world-view is based on the variation: "Shakespeare had a little secret." This we may term the **Radical Stratfordian** position. Within this umbrella are theories based on the idea that Shaksper-of-Stratford was indeed the author, but he had a secret life that shamed him, or was dangerous, and has thus never been verified. The most popular is the "Shakespeare was Gay" theory. Runners up are: "Shakespeare was a secret Catholic", "Shakespeare was a Spy", or "Shakespeare was a member of a Secret Society".

Venturing into un-orthodoxy completely we encounter the idea that "Shakespeare was really somebody else, but who knows who?" This is the classic **Anti–Stratfordian** paradigm. The 33 arguments against Shaksper's authorship of Shakespeare that I listed above have all been fleshed out into full explanations in countless books published in the last 100 years. There are many Anti–Stratfordians, and a good number of them are content to have the whole thing be a fine mystery, without yearning for a definitive answer.

The final stage is called **Heresy** or **Truth**, depending on your opinion. It is when one begins to make the claim, as I do in this book, that "Shakespeare was _____ " (fill in the blank). If you fill in the blank with Francis Bacon, you are a termed a *Baconian*; if you complete the equation with the Earl of Oxford, you are an *Oxfordian*.

# Chapter Four

# The Case for Oxford in Brief

The Oxford theory became widely known after the 1920 publication of *Shakespeare Identified*. Since then dozens of other books have been published advancing the Oxford theory. The most important are *This Star of England*, by Dorothy and Charlton Ogburn Sr., 1952; *Oxfordian Vistas*, by Ruth Lloyd Miller, 1975; *The Mysterious William Shakespeare, The Myth and the Reality*, by Charlton Ogburn Jr., 1984. The researchers of the Oxford theory have built on previous insights and have all made significant discoveries in the historical record that strengthen the case that de Vere wrote the Shakespeare plays. Throughout the 20th century, information leading to the identification of Oxford as Shakespeare has been accumulating at an accelerating rate, whereas the known facts concerning Shaksper-of-Stratford have grown hardly at all. This scant "new" information on Shaksper, such as his likely Catholic affiliations, can only weaken the argument that he wrote the Shakespeare Canon. The conventional case for attribution has hardly been improved, in spite of legions of graduate students poring through every available piece of paper.

## The most compelling evidence that Edward de Vere was Shakespeare

### 1. *Hamlet* tells the story of Oxford's life, down to the details.

Oxford's life was dramatically changed by the death of his father when he was young. Like Hamlet, young Oxford suffered the embarrassment of his mother's rapid remarriage. Though heir to an incredible Earldom, his estates were held by the Queen, though administered and exploited through the Court of Wards, Lord Burghley, and the Earl of Leicester. Oxford was a ward of the State, and was deprived of his rightful inheritance. As a young man in Burghley's household, Oxford accidentally killed a man in a sword fight, which appears to be echoed in *Hamlet*. Oxford kept a company of actors and wrote for them. In the play, Hamlet commandeers a group of players and alters their play to catch the conscience of the King.

**Polonius**, the statesman, and Hamlet's keeper, is the mirror of Lord Burghley, who was young Oxford's master and then his father-in-law. In the first edition of *Hamlet*, 1603, the Polonius character is called **Corambis**. Burghley's family motto was "Cor Unum Una Via" which means "One Heart, One Way." Thus "Cor-ambis" would mean "Wandering Heart". Lord Burghley was even referred to in his time as Polus, as in the Pole-Star around which everything else revolves. Polonius' famous admonitions to Hamlet consist of near verbatim expressions from Burghley's own private writings! We have this "smoking gun" of evidence because Burghley's advice, written before the 1590's to counsel his son Robert Cecil, were published in 1618, long after both father and son were dead. *Hamlet* first appeared in print in 1603. Shaksper-of-Stratford, who died in 1616, could not have had access to the Burghley's manuscript, published or unpublished. But Oxford, the real author of *Hamlet*, knew the Cecil family as well as anyone, having grown up in it, and married into it. The bulk of the surviving letters in Oxford's hand were addressed to either William or Robert Cecil.

Ophelia reflects Anne Cecil, the Countess Oxford, who also died unhappy, and too young. There is a Latin memorial to Anne Cecil Oxford which hints that despondency drove her to suicide by drowning. This potentially explosive evidence only remains inconclusive because suicide was a serious religious crime and no family would admit or permit speculation that a mysterious death was self inflicted. Hamlet entrusts his kinsman Horatio with carrying on his work, and telling his story. Oxford was survived in 1604 by his trusted first cousin Sir Horatio Vere, a noted military leader.

20

At the beginning of the play Hamlet meets the ghost of his father, and calls to him with the peculiar name "Truepenny". Oxford's Grandparents were Vere and Trussell. *Vere* is "True" and a *Trussell* was a press for minting pennies.

Hamlet calls Polonius a fishmonger. Burghley was quite notorious for putting a Bill through Parliament that added Wednesdays as a Fish day (no meat) in addition to traditional no-meat Fridays throughout England. This was to boost the fishing industry, and to Lord Burghley, who was heavily invested in it. When Lord Burghley's elder son Thomas Cecil was living in Paris, his father had spies reporting back to him about Thomas' gambling habit. This bit of private family history is manifest in *Hamlet* in Act II, where Polonius sends the spy Reynaldo to Paris to check on the habits of Polonius' son Laertes.

The book Hamlet is carrying around is *Cardanus Comfort*, the philosophical source of the "to be or not to be" soliloquy. The Earl of Oxford published *Cardanus Comfort* in English in 1573 and wrote a preface and a beautiful poem to accompany the work, which was a translation of the brilliant Italian mathematician and philosopher, Girolamo Cardano. The work is pictured on the next page. The title reads:

> Cardanus Comforte translated into Englishe.
> And published by commaundement of the right honourable the Earle of Oxenford.

From Cardano:
> What should we account of death to be resembled to anything better than sleep ? ...
> We are assured not only to sleep, but also to die...

The Earl of Oxford was abducted and robbed by pirates on a return trip to England. In the play, Hamlet is captured by pirates while en-route to England.

**Cardanus Comfort**, title page.

## 2. The personality profile of the author of the works matches de Vere's life.

In 1920, John Thomas Looney profiled the various human qualities and talents which the author of the Shakespeare plays would have had to possess, by characterizing the author through his interests and expertise, which fill the plays as sunlight fills space. By cataloging the knowledge and experience required to have conceived these plays and written such incredible texts, one can form a "profile" of the author through his evident obsessions. Looking objectively at the plays and poems, without preconception, one can be led to the following conclusions about the unknown Author:

1. He was man of recognized genius; a man of letters.
2. He was probably an eccentric or iconoclast.
3. He had an intense sensitivity. He was the world's greatest listener of people's actual talk.
4. He possessed an education in the Classics, and was especially fond of Ovid
5. He was involved professionally in the world of Drama and the theater.
6. He was a lyric poet, a songwriter, and probably a musician.
7. He had Aristocratic and Feudal sympathies.
8. He had access to the inner world of the Royal Court.
9. He was an enthusiast for all things Italian.
10. He was a Sportsman, a Horseman, a Falconer.
11. He was loose with money, not a miser or a saver.
12. He was very sexually aware, and polymorphously perverse.
13. He had a thorough knowledge of the Bible. He was a defender of the Church of England.
14. He had an intimate knowledge of soldiers and battles, seafaring, and pirates.
15. He had a profound knowledge of Law, and the English legal system.
16. He had a profound knowledge of cutting edge science, medicine, and Astronomy.
17. He had an intimate knowledge of English history.

Compared to all other candidates, Oxford gets the most hits.

Edward de Vere, 17th Earl of Oxford

Edward de Vere (April 12, 1550 - June 24, 1604) was born
into an ancient and prestigious family. The Vere Earls of
Oxford go back to the time of William the Conqueror. A

Vere was one of the original invaders in 1066, and his family received the feudal grants that became the Earldom of Oxford. These Earls were often king-makers, and the power near the throne of England.

Young Edward was tutored by the finest minds in England, including Sir Thomas Smith and Dr. Lawrence Nowell. He learned Latin under his maternal uncle Arthur Golding. At 12, he became a ward of the state, and went to live in the household of William Cecil, Lord Burghley. Oxford graduated Cambridge University, St. John's college, at the age of 14, in 1564. Two years later he received a Masters degree from Oxford University. He studied law at Gray's Inn and learned the intricacies of government, politics and litigation. He studied with the alchemist-astrologer Dr. John Dee. Oxford competed in Royal Tournaments and won. He married Burghley's daughter, Anne Cecil. Oxford traveled, without his wife, to the Continent in 1575-76, and was received with honor in France, Austria and Italy. His itinerary and whereabouts in Italy are extant. He was in Venice, and the other Italian locations in the Shakespeare plays. Back in England he became the patron of several theatrical companies. He brought the innovations of Italian theater to England. Oxford became a patron of Literature, encouraging translations, and sponsoring the talent of young playwrights. Contemporary books classed him as the greatest comic dramatist of his day, but in the standard story of history, Oxford's plays are "lost". They are not lost. They are the Shakespeare plays.

In the last decade of his life, Oxford and his second wife, Elizabeth Trentham retired to a London suburb called Hackney. Hackney is right down the road from England's *other* village of Stratford: Stratford-atte-Bowe as opposed to Stratford-on-Avon.

## 3. Oxford was actually referred to as a Spear Shaker in his own time.

Pallas Athene, the battle-ready goddess of philosophy, poetry, and the arts was also the patron of classical Greek Drama. Her Helmet of Invisibility allowed her privacy and the ability to see real life. Greek theater was dedicated to her and functioned under her protection. This theme was revived in Elizabethan England. "Pallas" from "pallein" means "to brandish or shake". Renamed as Minerva, she served the same role of patron of learning and drama for the Romans. She was known as "Hasti Vibrans" which means the "Spear-Shaker".

Harvey's encomiums of praise, title page.

In July, 1578, Queen Elizabeth and her Court traveled to Audley's End, in Cambridgeshire. Upon arrival the entourage was met and entertained by Gabriel Harvey, a writer, and fellow of Trinity College Cambridge. He addressed the Queen and her chief Courtiers with Latin encomiums of praise. It must have been excruciating for them all to sit through. Harvey's Latin speeches were published later that year in a lavish four-volume publication called *Gratulationis Valdinensis*. *Book Four (Liber Quartus)*, contains Harvey's encomiums to The Earl of Oxford, Christopher Hatton, and Philip Sidney.

**Vere family Coat of Arms.**

The Oxford section begins with the Coat of Arms of Edward de Vere. This is followed by a commentary on the Vere Motto (Vero Nihil Verius) displayed on the Arms. Harvey's conceit is called *Dialogus In Effigiem Nobilissimi Comitis Oxoniensis; illiusq; elegantissimum Symbolum: Vero Nil Verius.*

After some more dialog comes Harvey's poem of praise to Oxford.

> O great-hearted one, **strong in thy mind and thy fiery will**, thou wilt conquer thyself, thou wilt conquer others, thy glory will spread out in all directions …Do thou but go forward boldly and without hesitation. Mars will obey thee, Hermes will be thy messenger, **Pallas striking her shield with her spear shaft will attend thee**. For a long time past Phoebus Apollo has cultivated thy mind in the arts. **English poetical measures have been sung by thee long enough** …

> … **witness how greatly thou dost excel in letters**. I have seen many Latin verses of thine, yea, even more English verses are extant, **thou hast drunk deep draughts not only of the muses of France and Italy**, but hast learned the manners of many men, and the arts of foreign countries…

> In thy breast is noble blood, Courage animates thy brow,
> Mars lives in thy tongue, Minerva strengthens thy right hand,
> Bellona reigns in thy body, within thee burns the fire of Mars.
> Thine eyes flash fire,
> Thy will shakes spears
> Who would not swear that Achilles had come to life again?

The original is in Latin. The key words are:
Vultus Tela Vibrat

Vultus : will, intent, countenance
Tela :  spear, boar-spear
Vibrat : shakes

While the "usual" Latin word for spear is "hasta", the word **Tela** is used by Ovid for "Boar-spear" and is translated as such in the Elizabethan English version of *Metamorphoses*, credited to Oxford's uncle Arthur Golding, and already in print long before Harvey's poem. The credit goes to Andrew Hannas for this important discovery.

In Harvey's speech, note that he lauds Oxford with mastering the arts and culture of France and Italy, which would seem to be a prerequisite for being the person who wrote the Shakespeare plays.   Also in the encomium,

Harvey, apparently jealous of Oxford's blinding talent, encourages him to put down his pen and go to war:

> O thou hero worthy of renown, throw away the insignificant pen, throw away the bloodless books, and writings that serve no useful purpose; now must the sword be brought into play ...

Poetry and drama were officially considered frivolous trivialities in a culture that respected warriors more than entertainers. (Today we have the reverse). Oxford's paternal forbears were Heroes of England. He did desire to gain fame at war, but Queen Elizabeth never allowed him to get near any dangerous assignments. One theory is that Oxford's function as world-class entertainer to the Queen (as a dramatist and theatrical producer) was so important to her that she forbade him from assuming government or military assignments. Perhaps those writings did serve a useful purpose.

Edward de Vere held numerous titles including Lord Bulbek. The modern Bulbek Crest shows a Lion brandishing a broken spear. It has not yet been proved that this heraldic symbol was in use in the Elizabethan era. But it is another intriguing coincidence.

## 4. Oxford's published poetry shows a direct link to Shakespeare's.

Edward de Vere was well known in his day as an accomplished poet and dramatist. His work appeared in published poetry collections from the 1570's through his death in 1604. The modern *Palgrave's Golden Treasury* has a poem by de Vere.   So the question is not whether or not Oxford was a talented poet and writer, but whether his poetry and prose has echoes in Shakespeare.

### Grief of Mind

What plague is greater than the grief of mind?
The grief of mind that eats in every vein;
In every vein that leaves such clots behind;

Such clots behind as breed such bitter pain;
So bitter pain that none shall ever find
What plague is greater than the grief of mind.

Earl of Oxford, from *England's Parnassus*, 1600

Compare with Shakespeare:

DROMIO OF EPHESUS:
She is so hot because the meat is cold,
The meat is cold because you come not home,
 You come not home because you have no stomach,
You have no stomach, having broke your fast;
 But we, that know what 'tis to fast and pray,
Are penitent for your default to-day.
*Comedy of Errors* I, 2, 47-52

## 5. The Ashbourne Portrait of Shakespeare was an over-painting of an Oxford portrait.

This magnificent painting shows a nobleman in almost full length. The subject's right arm is resting atop a "memento mori" skull, his hand holding a gilt book with 4 red drawstrings. He wears a ring on the thumb of his left hand. For perhaps a century this painting was said to be Shakespeare, and when it came into the possession of the Folger Shakespeare Library it was prominently and proudly presented as a remarkable portrait of Shakespeare of Stratford-on-Avon.

There was quite a shock when Scientific American published an illustrated article on the Ashbourne Shakespeare, in the January, 1940 issue. The article reported that an X-ray analysis of the canvas had found that the image had been altered and over-painted. Identification of some of the hidden material: a boar's head on the thumb ring, and the Heraldic Arms of the Trentham family in the upper left portion of the painting, led researcher and author Charles Wisner Barrell to conclude that the sitter in the painting is Edward de Vere, the 17th Earl of Oxford.

At some point in the past 400 years someone severely re-
worked the portrait to make a man with a full head of hair

look something like the high-foreheaded cartoon image of Shakespeare from the *First Folio*.

X-ray analysis has shown that the original hairline had been raised by several inches. The subject in the painting wears a huge fluted courtiers ruff in the original. The over-painting reduces the ruff to gentleman's proportions and style. The forgers used gold paint to do the phony inscription in the upper left, Aetatis suae 47 Anno 1611, which gives a correct age for Shakespeare of Stratford, who was born in 1564. The same gold paint was used to alter the sitter's thumb ring, to highlight his belt, and to obliterate the markings on the book the man is holding. The X-ray of the thumb ring shows the remnant of a boar's head, the symbolic badge of the Earl of Oxford. Beneath the fake inscription at the upper left are the remains of a coat of arms that were nearly obliterated by the forgers. The identification of the correct family represented by the coat of Arms is still being debated. But the arms do match the family of Elizabeth Trentham, the Countess Oxford (de Vere's second wife.) The provenance of the painting also points to the Trenthams. The Ashbourne portrait emerged from the estate of Elizabeth Trentham Cockayne, the great-grand-niece of Elizabeth Trentham, the Countess of Oxford.

The initials C. K. in the lower right identify the painter as Cornelius Ketel, (1548-1616), the Dutch portrait artist. A contemporary account of Ketel's workshop from the year 1604, lists many portraits which Ketel had painted for Elizabethan dignitaries. A full size portrait of Oxford is listed in that account. Though the painting had been thought lost or destroyed, Barrell's identification in 1940 showed that The Ashbourne painting of Shakespeare is really an over-painting of the lost Ketel portrait of Oxford!

Since Barrell's work, the Ashbourne painting has been taken off general display, and the trustees of the Folger have mounted a counterattack that attempts to identify the sitter with a Mr. Hammersley of London. Of all the known portraits of Shakespeare, all but one are modeled on the *First*

*Folio* image. They all face left. Only the Ashbourne Portrait depicts the real person who was Shakespeare, and the proof is buried in the basement of the Folger Shakespeare Library of Washington DC.

## 6. The *Ovid's Metamorphoses* of Arthur Golding shows his nephew Oxford's hand.

*Ovid's Metamorphoses* was first translated into English in the early 1560's. The credit goes to Arthur Golding, a classical scholar, whose other translations are from the Bible, and the works of Calvin. It is a grand Literary mystery how Arthur Golding came to translate this bawdy Greek classic of pagan humanity and multiplicity of deity. And the translation itself is extravagant, childish, inventive, comical: everything that Golding's other work does not contain. Arthur Golding was Edward de Vere's maternal uncle. (Oxford's mother was Margery Golding).

The young Edward was under Golding's tutelage in Latin in exactly the same years that the *Metamorphoses* were translated and published. The work gets better, or more concise towards the end. The author got better as he was going along. Moreover, the wordiness, the playfulness, the taking of liberties with the project introduces language that includes personal references to young de Vere's surroundings, and observations about life. This vocabulary appears later in Oxford's letters and poems, and throughout the Shakespeare plays and poems.

The significance of *Metamorphoses* is that the standard story of the poet Shakespeare is that he was profoundly influenced by the Golding translation. The themes emerge over and over again, from *Venus & Adonis*, to *Midsummer Nights Dream*. "Shakespeare's favorite book" may actually have been written by the young Oxford. Translating the *Metamorphoses* as a young adult prodigy set the themes in motion that would catapult young de Vere into "Shakespeare".

**7. Oxford's annotated copy of the *Geneva Bible* marks passages that were used by Shakespeare.**

The Folger Library has in its collection a Geneva Bible, owned by the 17th Earl of Oxford, bearing his coat of arms, and underlined and briefly annotated throughout. Researcher Roger Stritmatter has studied the Oxford Geneva Bible, and compared the noted scriptural passages with the Biblical allusions throughout the Shakespeare plays and poems. The results are staggering. Prior scholarship had already determined that Shakespeare had been using a Geneva Bible, almost exclusively and obsessively. Books have appeared for a century finding Geneva passages in Shakespeare. Then this Oxford copy of the Geneva emerges, with the very passages predicted underlined, and more. Stritmatter found better examples of actual citations in Oxford's Geneva Bible than verses that were guessed at by the most orthodox scholars of Shakespeare and the Bible.

If the Bible at the Folger had Shaksper's name on it, instead of Oxford's, it would be held up as the Holy Grail of Shakespeare memorabilia. Not a single book owned by Shaksper has ever emerged ... and won't ever ... he didn't have any. Once again, the Folger has all the proof necessary locked in the vault, and continues to spin the fiction of the uneducated superman from Stratford who tossed off plays between buying and selling malt and barley. W. Shaksper was essentially a wholesale grocer.

**8. The Earl of Southampton ("Shakespeare's patron") has substantial links to the Earl of Oxford.**

The two long Shakespeare Poems, *Venus & Adonis*, 1593, and *The Rape of Lucrece*, 1594, both contain introductory dedications to Henry Wriothesley, the dashing young 3rd Earl of Southampton. Thus, in the traditional story, Southampton must have been "Shakespeare's Patron". But historians have been unable to connect Southampton to the man from Stratford-on-Avon and there has been nothing but conjecture as to what relationship, if any, the two men had.

However, because of the existence of those dedications, Southampton has to be dealt with in any complete "theory of Shakespeare". The Oxford Theory is very strong in this area.

Southampton was well known to Edward de Vere, the 17th Earl of Oxford. In the year 1593, Oxford was negotiating with the Wriothesley family for the marriage of his 17 year old daughter Elizabeth de Vere to the 20 year old Henry, Earl of Southampton. Southampton eventually rejected the marriage offer, but the correspondence extant proves that Oxford senior thought highly of young Wriothesley. They also shared in common a major life experience. Both Edward de Vere and Henry Wriothesley had lost their fathers as young men and were raised as Wards of the State in the household of William, Lord Burghley. In the 1600's Oxford's son Henry became a very close friend to Henry Wriothesley. They shared a passion for politics, theater, and military adventure.

The image below, which dates from 1624 or later, shows the two "Noble Henries", the Earls of Oxford and Southampton, riding horseback together in their co-command of the 6000 English troops in Holland that had joined with the Dutch forces in countering the continued attacks by Spain.

This picture serves as a reminder that a close relationship between the Vere family and Henry Wriothesley, Earl of Southampton, lasted for decades, and that Southampton *can* be linked historically to the author Shake-speare, provided that said author was really Edward de Vere.

**The two Henries.** Inscription at top left: *The Portraicture of the right honorableLords, the twomost noble HENRIES revived the Earles of Oxford and Southampton.* At top left: shield of Vere with motto: *Vero Nihil Verius.* In top right hand corner: shield of Wriothesley/Southampton. The motto on the banner above the shield reads: *Ung Par Tout, Tout Par Ung* (One for ll, all for one). The shield also displays the garter motto: *Honi Soit Qui Mal Y Pense.*

## 9. The Shakespeare First Folio of 1623 has links to Oxford's heirs and in-laws.

The *First Folio* has a dedication to the two brothers William Herbert, 3rd Earl of Pembroke, 1580-1630, and Philip Herbert,

1584-1650, (1ˢᵗ) Earl of Montgomery (and later the 4ᵗʰ Earl of Pembroke, after his brother's death.) Described in the *Folio* as "the most noble and incomparable pair of brethren", the Herbert brothers had risen to the top of Elizabethan politics after a long slow climb. Philip Herbert married Susan de Vere, the Earl of Oxford's daughter, in 1604, in an unbelievably lavish ceremony at Whitehall with King James and Court in attendance. Through Susan, who was a patron of Literature like her father, The Earl of Montgomery had access to Oxford's manuscripts. The Herbert brothers were also patrons of Ben Jonson, who seems to have served in some editorial capacity on the *First Folio* project. It is an interesting coincidence that the first publication of "Shakespeare's" collected Dramas, including 18 previously un-printed Shakespeare plays, occurred during the era when William Herbert, Earl of Pembroke, served as Lord Chamberlain of England, from 1615 to 1626. As Lord Chamberlain, Pembroke had control over all aspects of theater, drama, and entertainment, including the issuing of plays. As the content of the Shakespeare plays is so stridently open-minded, poly-religious, poly-sexual, bawdy, bloody, philosophical, and political, the publication of the *Folio* in 1623 against the backdrop of rising Puritanism and intense factionalism is near miraculous.

Because the Herberts were directly related to the Veres, and Henry de Vere, 18ᵗʰ Earl of Oxford was an ambitious and powerful politician and military hero in 1623, printing the plays with the name Edward de Vere on the cover would have been political suicide for everyone involved. With the plays revealed as coming from a court insider, the allusions to persons still alive would be shocking and unacceptable. By putting the "blame", the "fame", and the "Name" on the already deceased William Shaksper of Stratford, who had once "fronted" for Oxford 26 years earlier, the works could be published for posterity (and for profit) without any of the many aristocratic relatives of the Vere's having their reputations damaged.

There is also a political aspect to the publication of the *First Folio* of Shakespeare. Researcher Peter Dickson has outlined, in a series of articles, the significance of a major State political rivalry, involving King James and his favorite Buckingham on one side, and Oxford's son Henry de Vere, the 18th Earl, Henry Wriothesley, 3rd Earl of Southampton, and William Herbert, Earl of Pembroke. The proposed dynastic marriage between Prince Charles and the Spanish Princess Infanta Maria, (the little sister of King Philip III of Spain) was supported by the King, Buckingham, and those who favored a peaceful alliance with Spain. If the marriage had occurred, England might have folded back into the Catholic Church. The marriage was proposed in 1617, but it wasn't until 1621 that Prince Charles (the future doomed King Charles I of England) traveled with Buckingham to Spain. The shocker was that Charles actually fell in love with Infanta Maria and the whole fake marriage deal started to get real.

The most vocal opponents of the Spanish match were the two Henries, Oxford and Southampton. Because of their overt resistance, Henry de Vere and Southampton were imprisoned in 1621. After a release, Henry de Vere was arrested again and was on "death row" in the Tower of London from April 1622 to December 1623. The 18th Earl of Oxford was in the Tower during the entire time the *Folio* was being prepared. To complete this incredible story, in November of 1623, Southampton, who was not in prison, made a public reconciliation with Buckingham and cut a deal for the release of Henry de Vere. On November 8, 1623, the Shakespeare *Folio* plays were registered in the Stationers' Company, the book having been printed by that date. Within a year both Southampton and Oxford died mysteriously and suddenly.

**10. Oxford was deeply involved in the theater and his "missing Plays" aren't missing.**

Oxford's contemporaries classed him as a brilliant poet, and the greatest comic dramatist, but the majority of his works seem to have gone "missing in action", and disappeared from history.

In the 1586 book, *A Discourse on English Poesy*, William Webbe wrote:

> I may not omit the deserved commendations of many honourable and noble Lords and Gentlemen in Her Majesty's Court, which, **in the rare devises of poetry have been and yet are most skillful; among whom the right honourable Earl of Oxford may challenge to himself the title of most excellent among the rest.**

In 1589, the anonymous book, *The Art of English Poesie* documented the esteem in which Oxford was held by his contemporaries, and the masking of identity that was required due to the social conventions of the era.

Among the nobility or gentry as may be very well seen in many laudable sciences and especially in making poesie, it is so come to pass that they have no courage to write & if they have, are loath to be known of their skill. **So as I know very many notable gentleman in the Court that have written commendably, and suppressed it again, or else suffered it to be published without their own names to it: as it were a discredit for a gentleman, to seem learned."**

And in Her Majesty's time that now is, are sprung up another crew of Courtly makers, Nobleman and Gentlemen of Her Majesty's own servants, **who have written excellently well, as it would appear *if their doings could be found out and made public with the rest*, of which number is first that noble gentleman Edward Earl of Oxford.**

### Oxford and the Theater

Oxford's association with the theater was inherited from his family. The Earls of Oxford kept acting companies as far back as 1492. John Bale (1495-1563), was a Protestant reformer, a writer, and early English dramatist. John Bale was connected to both the 15th and 16th Earls of Oxford, and was even a familiar figure to young Edward de Vere, the future 17<sup>th</sup> Earl, born 1550.

In a 1536 account, Bale noted the titles, and the first lines, of fourteen plays which he had written on commission for John de Vere, the 15<sup>th</sup> Earl of Oxford. One of these plays is called *King John*! In 1561, Queen Elizabeth was entertained at Castle Hedingham by John, 16<sup>th</sup> Earl of Oxford, who supported a troupe of actors. Young Oxford was there and perhaps had his first opportunity to entertain his Queen.

Edward de Vere took the family fascination with drama a step further, by actually writing and producing plays and entertainments. As a student at Gray's Inn, he took part in its hallowed tradition of amateur theatrical productions. In Italy, Oxford learned the innovations of Renaissance drama, and brought them back to England. The idea that a character could have and describe inner conflicts and emotions was born. Oxford staged outdoor extravaganzas to amuse the Queen and Court. One time the pyrotechnics got out of control and a building caught fire.

Oxford supported, with money and lodgings, a series of dramatists who are normally considered "Shakespeare's predecessors". Anthony Munday, George Peele, John Lyly, and Robert Greene all benefited from de Vere's patronage and his themes can be seen in their early productions. When they were out of favor and employment with Oxford, their material suddenly becomes soggy and all wit disappears. The early works produced by Oxford and his University Wits contain many of the plots seen handled much more expertly in the mature Shakespeare plays.

## Oxford and the Blackfriars Theater

In *The Merry Wives of Windsor* the Welshman Hugh Evans is a transparent representation of the Earl of Oxford's theater manager, Henry Evans, a Welshman who was the teacher and Master of the Children of Paule's troupe. In *Merry*

*Wives*, Sir Hugh rehearses the children in the Fairy masque which ends the play.

The real man, Henry Evans, started out as a scrivener and theatrical hanger on. In the years 1584 - 1586 the Earl of Oxford arranged to lease a large hall in the Blackfriars building in London as a playhouse. Oxford also leased the downstairs to serve as a top flight fencing school. There is a complicated paper trail on this that still exists, and there are payments to connect Oxford as the patron, John Lyly as go-between and proprietor, and Henry Evans as theater manager. Their troupe of young actors was created by combining the Children of Paul's with the Children of the Chapel. The combined group was often referred to as Oxford's Boys. They were not just making random entertainments; throughout the 1580's they were performing for the Queen and her Court and to private audiences.

## Oxford and the Boar's Head Theater

Near the end of the reign of Queen Elizabeth, the theaters were getting themselves into trouble and were frequently shut down. In March of 1602, the Earl of Oxford and the Earl of Worcester were allowed to combine their acting companies and were granted special rights to continue to perform plays. Their venue was the Boar's Head Inn, which had been converted into a theater. The Boar's Head Inn, on Hogs Lane in Whitechapel, was just outside the City Limits of London. This special dispensation allowed for the dramatic activities to continue, even though they had been banned in London. The name of the theater is significant, because of the frequent mentions of a Boar's Head tavern in the Shakespeare plays, and also because the Boar's Head, a Blue Boar, was Oxford's family badge.

## Oxford's "Lost Plays"

There is an interesting curiosity in the paper trail.

A list of Plays produced for Queen Elizabeth in the 1570's and 1580's exists and the titles of some of the anonymous plays produced by the Paul's Boys, the Lord Chamberlain's Men, and Oxford's Men is fascinating. During the era of these productions, Oxford's total involvement with the theater was uncomplicated by other responsibilities. During this period Oxford was also busy selling off estates to keep cash flow, and creditors at bay.

The chart below shows the early plays associated with Oxford's patronage, which have titles suggestive of later model "Shakespearean" plays.

| Date | Company with Oxford link | Title |
|---|---|---|
| Jan. 1, 1577 | Children of Paul's | The History of Error |
| Feb. 17, 1577 | Lord Chamberlain's Men | History of the Solitary Knight |
| Feb. 19, 1577 | Children of Paul's | Titus and Gisippus |
| Dec. 28, 1578 | Lord Chamberlain's Men | Cruelty of a Stepmother |
| Jan. 1, 1579 | Children of Paul's | Marriage of Mind and Measure |
| Jan. 6, 1579 | Lord Chamberlain's Men | Rape of the Second Helen |
| Jan. 11, 1579 | Lord Chamberlain's Men | Mask of Amazons and Knights |
| Mar. 3, 1579 | Lord Chamberlain's Men | Murderous Michael |
| Dec. 26, 1579 | Lord Chamberlain's Men | Duke of Milan and Marquis of Mantua |
| Feb. 2, 1580 | Lord Chamberlain's Men | Portio and Demorantes |
| Dec. 27, 1584 | Oxford's Boys | Agamemmnon and Ulysses |

In her 1931 book, *Hidden Allusions in Shakespeare's plays*, Eva Turner Clark, was the first to offer speculation as to what plays these Antique dramas evolved into:

| | | |
|---|---|---|
| The History of Error | = | The Comedy of Errors |
| History of the Solitary Knight | = | Timon of Athens |
| "Titus Andgisippus" | = | Titus Andronicus |
| Cruelty of a Stepmother | = | Cymbeline |
| Marriage of Mind and Measure | = | Taming of the Shrew |
| Rape of the Second Helen | = | All's Well that End's Well |
| Mask of Amazons and Knights | = | Love's Labours Lost |
| Murderous Michael | = | Arden of Feversham (Shakespeare Apocrypha) |
| Duke of Milan & Marquis of Mantua | = | Two Gentlemen of Verona |
| Portio and Demorantes | = | Merchant of Venice |
| Agamemmnon and Ulysses | = | Troilus & Cressida |

## 11. Blatant hints in the plays and poems themselves relate to key events in Oxford's life.

### All's Well that Ends Well

The scholarly *Arden Shakespeare* edition of *All's Well* has, in the introductory section, a sub-chapter which discusses "the bed trick" which serves as a plot device in the play. The bed-trick in essence is that a man is tricked into sleeping with his own wife, after another woman woos him, arranges a rendezvous, and then is replaced by the wife, wearing the temptress' clothing, in a dark midnight setting. The Arden editor actually cites the legends surrounding the Earl of Oxford as proof that the bed-trick was a viable thing to be joking about.

A 1658 book, *Memoires*, by Francis Osborne gives this gossip:

> ... the last great Earle of Oxford, whose Lady was brought to his bed under the notion of his Mistress, and from such a virtuous deceit she <a daughter> is said to proceed.

Osborne's account was probably based on the existing letters and memoranda which touch on the occasion of the birth of Oxford's first daughter Elizabeth, by Anne Cecil Oxford, on July 2, 1575. Oxford was out of the country and learned of his wife's pregnancy in the mail. He did not learn the actual date of his daughter's birth until later. When he did the math, he figured he might not be the father. Oxford and Anne were estranged for several years, and Oxford would not see his young daughter. Eventually a rumor was hatched that Oxford had indeed slept with his wife on the appropriate night, but he had been tricked into it, and that is why he didn't remember right off the bat. All was apparently forgiven, Edward and Anne reunited and had several more children together.

In *All's Well*, the hero Bertram, like Oxford, loses his father and is brought up as a royal ward. Helena is a ward to the countess, and the daughter of a famous doctor. Helena is in love with Bertram but feel she is too low to win his hand in

43

marriage. When the match between Oxford and Anne Cecil was proposed, they had already lived together in the same household, as virtually brother and sister. Anne was, in fact, "too low" to marry Oxford. In order for the marriage to proceed, the Cecil family was granted nobility; that is, William Cecil was created "Lord Burghley" by Queen Elizabeth, to reward Cecil, and to cement a direct access to Oxford's huge inheritance of encumbered properties.

Helena is introduced in the play as the daughter of Gerard de Narbonne, who is described as a master healer and herbalist. The ailing King of France has tried every cure for his mystery ailment, and finally agrees to be treated by Helena, with her miraculous medicine. She cures him, and is offered marriage to Bertram as a reward. Bertram reluctantly marries her, then runs off to war. Oxford ran away when he got married, too. The healer Gerard is mentioned at least 3 times. The name comes from the sources (*Pallace of Pleasure* and *The Decameron* ) but its repetition emphasizes the name of John Gerard, Burghley's gardener, and the premier Herbalist / Healer in England. The young Edward de Vere likely spent countless hours learning botany and plants directly from John Gerard. Shakespeare is noted for his incredible knowledge of plants, and plant lore. Interestingly, a majority of Shakespeare's favorite flowers are prominent in East Anglia, where de Vere lived, but not in Warwickshire where Shaksper lived.

In Act III, the Clown says he knows a man so in love with music that he sold a manor for a song.

CLOWN:      I know a man that had this trick of melancholy sold a
            goodly manor for a song.
            *All's Well* Act III, Scene 2

The Earl of Oxford **did** lease or sell a manor to his friend William Byrd, the master Lutenist and composer, for an incredibly low price. Oxford was closely associated with Byrd, with John Dowland, and with John Farmer, the premiere music makers in England. They praised Oxford for his patronage, and his own musical and songwriting abilities. It has long been thought that Shakespeare, whoever he was, must have been an adept musician and songwriter because of the depth of the use of music in all the plays, and the lyrical beauty of the "Shakespeare Songs" (which are actually de Vere's songs).

A special ring is given by Helena to Bertram, who then gives it back in the bed-trick. It is documented that Oxford and Anne exchanged engraved rings before he left for his Continental tour.

The scenes in which the soldier Parolles is interrogated match aspects of the Howard-Arundel-Oxford Documents, a huge cache of depositions in which three ranking Earls of the realm accused each other of the highest and lowest crimes imaginable. During the interrogation, Parolles says:

PAROLLES: I humbly thank you, sir. **A truth's a truth** ...

*All's Well*, Act IV, Scene 3

The Oxford's family motto is Vero Nihil Verius, ... **There is nothing as True as the Truth.**

*All's Well that Ends Well* is so personal to Oxford that it is not surprising that it was one of the "lost" or "held back" plays that was publicly unknown until 1623. Incredibly, the first known **public** performance of *All's Well* wasn't until 1741! But, if E.T. Clark's theory is correct, *All's Well* was originally called *The Rape of the Second Helen*, and was performed for the Queen and Court by the Lord Chamberlains Men in 1579, when the topical humor was contemporary to the actual estrangement and reconciliation of Oxford and his wife, the Countess Anne.

## The Italian Plays

Oxford's year in Italy gave him the deep background necessary to write the plays with Italian settings. On Oxford's Continental tour of 1575, he first went to Paris where he met the new King, and had a portrait painted that he sent back to England to his wife. Oxford then traveled to Strasbourg where he met with the scholar Sturmius. De Vere continued on to Italy. "For fear of the Inquisition I dare not pass by Milan, the Bishop whereof exerciseth such tyranny," Oxford wrote from **Padua** to his father-in-law Lord Burghley. After Padua he traveled to Genoa and Venice. From the existing records of his stay in Italy we learn that Lord Oxford had occasion to borrow 500 crowns from a man named **Baptista** Nigrone; a few months later borrowed more crowns from a money-man named Pasquino **Spinola**. In *The Taming of the Shrew* **Baptista Minola** is the name of Katharina's father. He is obsessed with his "crowns". *Taming of the Shrew* is set in **Padua**.

The "shrew" in *Taming of the Shrew*, Katherina, is thought to be modeled in part on Edward de Vere's older sister Katherine de Vere Windsor. Sister Kate sued her brother Edward, and tried to get his entire inheritance and Earldom taken away, when he was only a teenager. She did not succeed, but clearly, he did not forget the experience.

One of the plot sources of *The Merchant of Venice* is the English book, *Zelauto*, 1580, credited to Anthony Munday, who was then Oxford's secretary. In fact *Zelauto* is a lavish production and is dedicated in full to Edward de Vere, 17th Earl of Oxford.

The Trial scenes in *Merchant of Venice* have the ring of authenticity. Scholars have noted an echo in Portia's speech of the heartfelt plea voiced by Mary Queen of Scots at her own trial. Edward de Vere was one of the judges in Mary's Trial.

*Romeo & Juliet* is based on an Italian folktale, and a poem in English, *Romeus & Juliet*, from 1562. But the clan warfare and fight scenes are based on Oxford's own experiences. In 1580, Oxford had an affair with one of the Queen's maids of honor, Anne Vavasour. Anne got pregnant and bore Oxford a son, (one who could never be an heir, Sir Edward Vere). The affair had repercussions, including both Oxford and Vavasour being imprisoned for a spell, and Vavasour's relatives, the Howards staging a vendetta with gang attacks on Oxford's men.

Oxford himself took part in one street skirmish and was wounded severely. Interestingly, in the play, Romeo is a Montague. Oxford himself had ancestors who were illustrious members of the English family of Montagues.

## The Merry Wives of Windsor

Shakespeare's play, *The Merry Wives of Windsor*, set in the environs of Windsor Castle, weaves a street level story of love, lust, greed, competition and humiliation. In the opening, bored pathetic Slender wishes he had his copy *of Songes & Sonnets*. This watershed book of poetry in the English language was written by Edward de Vere's poet uncle, Henry Howard, the Earl of Surrey (c. 1517 – 1547). *Songes and Sonnets*, the first edition of Surrey's poetry, was published posthumously as a miscellany by Richard Tottel in 1557, when Oxford was seven. The martyred Surrey was the husband of Frances de Vere, Oxford's paternal aunt, so it is reasonable to conjecture that the life and creative work of this uncle were a major influence on a boy who grew up to write some pretty good Sonnets himself, all in the style popularized by Surrey. The book was such a hit that it was immediately reprinted, and before the year was out the book was reset into a second edition. Its enduring popularity is attested to by the fact that it was reprinted frequently over three decades. There were quarto editions of *Songes and Sonnets* in 1559, 1565, 1567, two in 1574, 1585, and 1587. But after the 1587 edition there were no further reprints until the 19th century. Look at the dates. *Songes and Sonnets* was brought back into a commercial revival in the time era 1585 -1587. There were, however, no editions published during the 1590's or in 1602, when the supposed composition and audience for *Merry Wives* are conventionally dated. The topical allusion to Surrey's poetry would not be particularly meaningful to a 1602 audience. For this and other reasons, a mid 1580's date for the writing and first production of *Merry Wives* makes more sense.

The Author of *Merry Wives* slips in the name "Vere" three times through the context of the heavily-accented French Doctor asking where people are : "Vere is _____ ?" In one case, the joke has an extra punch:

CAIUS      Oui; mette le au mon pocket: depeche, quickly. **Vere is dat knave, Rugby**?

QUICKLY    What, John Rugby? John!
     Act 1, scene 4

"Rugby" as a word brings up only one connotation to modern readers : the energetic football game. But "Rugby" the game name, dates only from the nineteenth century when the game was invented at the Rugby School. Rugby, in Warwickshire, is a football kick away from Bilton manor on the Avon. Bilton manor was brought into the Oxford estates when John de Vere, the 15th Earl of Oxford, married Elizabeth Trussel. When Edward de Vere's father John, the 16th Earl died, Bilton was one of the estates left in trust to provide income for Margery Golding de Vere, his widow (Oxford's mother). So John Rugby is apt, if Edward's father or grandfather is implied. The simplest solution of the "Rugby" riddle, the continuous references to John Rugby in Merry Wives, is that they are allusions to one of the Earls of Oxford named John, associated with Bilton near Rugby.

The character who is nearly cuckolded is Master Ford. Through much of the comedy he is disguised and doing deception as "Master Brooke." At the end of the play, Falstaff, adorned with huge antlers, has been publicly humiliated by his reaction to the fairy display. Mr. Ford tells Falstaff that because of his horns, he (Falstaff) is both an ass and an Ox. Ford's exact wordplay suggests he himself is an Ox-Ford, too:

MRS. FORD:    Sir John, we have had ill luck; we could never meet. I will never take you for my love again; but I will always count you my deer.

FALSTAFF:    I do begin to perceive that I am made an ass.

FORD:    **Ay, and an ox too**; both the proofs are extant.

Throughout the play Master Ford makes a big show of fearing he will grow cuckold-horns himself, a suggestive pun for Oxford, whose contretemps with his wife and her family over the rumor that she had cuckolded him while he was away in Italy was made, as he termed it, "the fable of the world". This Ox-Ford assumes the identity of "Brooke," a ruse to determine the strength of his wife's fidelity, by trying to seduce her while dressed as another man.

An obscure man named Arthur Brooke, who died at a young age, received the credit for the 1562 poem *Romeus & Juliet*, an acknowledged source for the later Shakespeare play. Yet, there are significant indications that young Oxford wrote the poem himself, and used the convenient name of his deceased contemporary. The point relative to *Merry Wives* is that Oxford had quite possibly used the name of Master Brooke himself, years earlier. The Arthur Brooke of fame is recorded as having died at sea. The motif of falling into the water is also echoed *in Merry Wives* when Falstaff, hiding in a laundry basket, is heaved into the Thames. If the name of Brooke as the cover-name for Master Ford were just an innocent, random choice, it is hard to explain why the name Brooke was changed to "Broome" when *Merry Wives* was re-edited for the *First Folio* in 1623. In the *Folio*, with Brooke switched into Broome, the many water puns are lost. For this reason why most stage productions use Master "Brooke," the name from the quarto.

In a scenario developed in detail by both J. T. Looney and Ruth Lloyd Miller, **Ann Page** represents the teen-aged Anne Cecil, who became the young wife of Edward de Vere. In the opinion of these leading Oxfordian scholars, the primary subtext of Merry Wives is a nostalgic review of the courtship or rivalry for the hand of young Anne Cecil, before she became Oxford's wife.

Edward de Vere knew Anne, long before he became engaged to her. For Edward had been a ward of the state since the age of twelve, and in the custody of William Cecil. Anne Cecil and Edward de Vere may have had a brother-sister relationship initially, simply out of proximity. Anne was thirteen years old in 1569 when her father, (who was still "Sir William", and not yet ennobled into Lord Burghley), began fishing for a rich, high-ranking husband for Anne. Negotiations took place with Sir Philip Sidney's father with regard to a marriage between their children. Young Philip also was long acquainted with Anne, as he had often been a guest at Cecil House in the 1560's and was admitted to Gray's Inn, also overseen by Cecil, in 1567, where he became young Oxford's classmate. Sidney and Oxford were thus rivals in school, in poetry, and in the competition for Anne. For Sidney, the financial rewards of marrying Anne would be greater than her gain from accepting him. Sidney was personally upset to lose Anne to Oxford, who could have sought any woman in Christendom. In *Merry Wives*, Oxfordians see a reflection of Philip Sidney in the youthful suitor Slender, while Oxford is represented by Fenton. With Sidney as Slender, Slender's uncle, the unscrupulous Justice Robert Shallow, can be seen as Sidney's uncle, the powerful Robert Dudley, Earl of Leicester, who as the Queen's favorite, was a law unto himself in England. In the real events, the scheming to link the Dudley-Sidney family faction to the Cecils featured wooing by the grownups on behalf of young Sidney. Philip Sidney was "slender" not only because he was skinny, but also because of his slender finances: he had no money. In the play, Slender's relatives put up land as security to offer Anne a dowry in the form of a jointure worth hundreds of pounds per annum. There are several specific "dollar figures" in the play regarding marriage payments, all of which dovetail with actual numbers in the extant Sidney-Cecil negotiations for the hand of young Anne.

Slender says (Act 1, scene 1 ) that he will be poor "till my mother be dead." The surviving documents show that Sidney's accounting of future assets which could be offered to Anne Cecil included the fact that he would inherit a huge amount of money if his mother died, but only a moderate inheritance if the father died. In *Merry Wives* it is only Fenton who directly courts Anne, and who also understands that he must negotiate with her father.

Even if the marriage between Oxford and Anne was arranged from above, and Oxford had no initial romantic interest in her, there is evidence from Cecil's letters that young Oxford pursued Anne by negotiating directly with William Cecil.

There is an odd exchange involving Dr. Caius that gives a comic clue to Anne Page's identity. Dr. Caius is the third suitor to Anne Page, and to get him out of the way he is told to meet Anne, ready to elope, at Herne's Oak where she will be dressed in green, so that Caius is tricked into running off with a boy dressed in green. Then, after Caius has been snookered:

MRS. PAGE:    Good George, be not angry. I knew of your purpose; turn'd my daughter into green; and, indeed, she is now with the Doctor at the dean'ry, and there married.

CAIUS:    **Vere is Mistress Page**? By gar, I am cozened; I ha' married un garcon, a boy; un paysan, by gar a boy; it is not Anne Page; by gar, I am cozened.

**Fenton** is described in the play both as a gentleman, and a noble. In Act III, scene 2, Page says of Fenton: "The gentleman is of no having: he kept company with the wild Prince and Poins; he is of too high a region, he knows too much. "Too high a region" can only refer to an aristocrat. Fenton himself says : "I am too great of birth" (Act III, scene 4).

Fenton speaks poetry, he has a wild past, and though he is low on cash, he is one also who, amazingly, ends up outwitting the other suitors to Anne Page, and wins her hand in marriage in the final scene. As one watches the play unfold, audiences are astounded that Shakespeare would give the prize to Fenton. Fenton "smells of April and May" ( that is, he is "spring-like," or "Ver"). Interestingly, there was a real person of the era named Fenton who was known by William Cecil, Oxford and Anne. Geoffrey Fenton was stationed in Ireland from 1580 to 1585, and his letters to Walsingham and Cecil are extant.

Fenton also dedicated one of his books to Anne Cecil de Vere, the Countess Oxford. The work is entitled: *Golden*

51

*Epistles, containing variety of discourse gathered as well out of the remainder of Guevara's works, as other authors, Latin, French, and Italian.* The first edition was printed in 1575, and the book was popular enough to be reprinted in 1577, and again in 1582. Fenton also wrote material that was "used by Shakespeare." The book, *Certaine Tragicall Discourses of Bandello*, 1567, is cited by Bullough as a likely source for *Othello*.

In *Merry Wives*, the character Fenton sounds quite like young Oxford, Cecil's ward.

FENTON:        I see I cannot get thy father's love;
                    Therefore no more turn me to him, sweet Nan.

ANNE:          Alas, how then?

FENTON.:      Why, thou must be thyself.
                    He doth object **I am too great of birth**;
                    And that, **my state being gall'd with my expense**,
                    I seek to heal it only by his wealth.
                    Besides these, other bars he lays before me,
                    My riots past, my wild societies;
                    And tells me 'tis a thing impossible
                    I should love thee but as a property.
                    (Act 3, scene 4)

ANNE:          May be he tells you true.

HOST:          What say you to young Master Fenton? He capers, he dances, he has eyes of youth, **he writes verses**, he speaks holiday, he smells April and May; he will carry 't, he will carry 't; 'tis in his buttons; he will carry 't.

PAGE:          Not by my consent, I promise you. The gentleman is of no having: **he kept company with the wild Prince and Poins; he is of too high a region, he knows too much**. No, he shall not knit a knot in his fortunes with the finger of my substance; if he take her, let him take her simply; the wealth I have waits on my consent, and my consent goes not that way.          (Act 3, Scene 2)

Portraying Fenton as one of the associates of Poins and Prince Hal links him to the Boar's Head Tavern gang in Henry IV part 1. The Gads Hill incident of the Henry play, so closely modeled on an actual skirmish in Oxford's early life, furthers the identification of Fenton with Oxford. It is also noteworthy that Oxford's Men, an adult troupe from the late '90s, last played the Boar's Head in 1602, the year *Merry Wives* was first published.

No single character in *Merry Wives* is exclusively Oxford. As a suitor he is Fenton,  as a jealous husband he is Ford/Brooke.  As a weary philosopher and bawd, he speaks as Falstaff.

## 12. Oxford's published prose and Oxford's letters show Shakespeare's language and philosophy.

One of the problems with the standard view of Shakespeare is that there are no documents in his hand, no letters, loose notes, rough drafts, or even laundry lists. But when Oxford is considered as a candidate for Authorship, there is a wealth of Oxford - penned material which can be compared to the known works of Shakespeare. There are more than 70 surviving Oxford letters, several published introductions, much published poetry, and legal documents as well. Many of these Oxford documents contain language so blindingly similar to Shakespeare that it is hard not to see the continuity of theme and voice.

From Oxford's introduction to *Cardanus Comfort*, 1573 :

Again we see, if our friends be dead, we cannot show or declare our affection more than by erecting them of tombs, whereby,  when they be dead indeed, yet we make them live, as again, through their monument ... But with me behold it happeneth far better, for in your lifetime I shall erect you such a monument that, as I say, in your lifetime, you shall see how noble a shadow of your virtuous life shall hereafter remain when you are dead and gone. And in your lifetime, again I say, I shall give you that monument and remembrance of your life whereby I may declare my good will...

Oxford at age 23 (1573)

"Remembrance" is a favorite word of Shakespeare, the coiner of the phrase "remembrance of things past" in Sonnet 30:

> When to the sessions of sweet silent thought,
> I summon up remembrance of things past ...

*The Sonnets* were written no earlier than the 1590's. Here the mature writer deals with the theme:

> Your name from hence immortal life shall have,
> Though I (once gone) to all the world must die,
> The earth can yield me but a common grave,
> When you entombed in men's eyes shall lie,
> Your monument shall be my gentle verse,
> Which eyes not yet created shall o'er-read,
> And tongues to be, your being shall rehearse,
> When all the breathers of this world are dead,

From Sonnet 81

| | |
|---|---|
| Bene. | An old, an old instance, Beatrice, that liv'd in the time of good neighbours. If a man do not erect in this age his own tomb ere he dies, he shall live no longer in monument than the bell rings and the widow weeps. |

*Much Ado*, Act V, Scene 2

Oxford's repeated cliché "as I say", may seem annoying, but it is a device that appears often in the plays:

| | |
|---|---|
| POMPEY. | No, indeed, sir, not of a pin; you are therein in the right; but to the point. **As I say**, this Mistress Elbow, being, **as I say**, with child, and being great-bellied, and longing, **as I said**, for prunes; and having but two in the dish, **as I said**, Master Froth here, this very man, having eaten the rest, **as I said**, and, **as I say**, paying for them very honestly; for, as you know, Master Froth, I could not give you three pence again. |

*Measure For Measure* Act II scene 1

Tis a chough; but, as I say, spacious in the possession of dirt.

## *Hamlet* Act V, Scene 2

In another section of Oxford's 1573 introduction to *Cardanus Comfort* he writes:

> What doth avail the vine unless another delighteth in the grape?
>
> What doth avail the rose unless another took pleasure in the smell?
>
> Why should this tree be accounted better than that tree but for the goodness of his fruit?
>
> Why should this rose be esteemed than that rose, unless in the pleasantness of smell it far surpassed the other rose?

## From *Romeo and Juliet*, published 24 years later:

Juliet :   What's Montague? it is nor hand, nor foot,
Nor arm, nor face, nor any other part belonging to a man.
O, be some other name!
What's in a name? That which we call a rose
by any other name would smell as sweet.
*R&J* Act II, Scene 2

## From Oxford's Letter to Sir Robert Cecil; April 25-27, 1603, discussing the death of Elizabeth:

**I cannot but** find a **great grief** in myself, to remember **the mistress which** we have lost, under whom both you and myself **from our greenest years have been in a manner brought up**. And although it hath pleased god, after an **earthly** kingdom, to take her up into a more permanent and **heavenly** state, wherein I do not doubt but she is crowned with glory, and to give us **a prince wise, learned, and enriched with all virtues**, yet the **long time which we spent in her service**, we cannot look for so much left of our days, as to bestow upon an other, **neither the long aquaintance, and kind familiarities,** wherewith she did use us, we are not ever to expect from another prince, as denied by **the infirmity of age**, and **common course of reason.**

In this **common shipwreck**, mine is above all the rest. Who least regarded, though often comforted, of all her followers, she hath left to **try my fortune** among the alterations of time, [fortune] and chance, either without **sail whereby to take the advantage of any prosperous gale**, or without anchor to ride till the storm be over past. ...

Your assured friend and unfortunate Brother in Law
E. Oxenford

## From Shakespeare:

QUEEN:        **I cannot but** be sad; so heavy sad
As-though, on thinking, on no thought I think-
Makes me with heavy nothing faint and shrink...
*Richard II*, Act II, Scene 2

CONSTANCE:  To me, and to the state of my **great grief**,
Let kings assemble; for my **grief's so great**
That no supporter but the huge firm earth can hold it up.
*King John*, Act III, Scene 1

FERDINAND:  This my mean task would be as heavy to me as odious,
But **the mistress which I serve** quickens what's dead,
And makes my labours pleasures.
*The Tempest* Act III. Scene1

KING:        I entreat you both that, being of so young days brought
up with him,
And since so neighbour'd to his youth and haviour,
That you vouchsafe your rest here in our court some
little time ...
*Hamlet*, Act II, Scene 2

And were I not immortal, life were done
Between this **heavenly** and **earthly** sun
*Venus and Adonis* line # 198

ESCALUS:    I am sorry **one so learned and so wise as you, Lord**
Angelo, have still appear'd, should slip so grossly, both
in the heat of blood and lack of temper'd judgment
afterward.
*Measure for Measure* Act V, Scene 1

CRANMER:   All **princely** graces that mould up such a mighty piece
as this is,
**With all the virtues** that attend the good, shall still be
doubled on her.

MALCOLM.       We shall not **spend a large expense of time** before we
               reckon with your several loves and make us even with
               you.
               *Macbeth* Act V, Scene 9


SLENDER.       … if there be no great love in the beginning, yet heaven
               may decrease it upon better **acquaintance**, when we are
               married and have more occasion to know one another. I
               hope upon **familiarity** will grow more contempt.
               *Merry Wives*, Act I, Scene 1


REGAN:         'Tis **the infirmity of his age**; yet he hath ever but
               slenderly known himself.
               *King Lear* Act I, Scene 1


1st LORD:      Merely our own traitors. And as **in the common course
               of all treasons** we still see them reveal themselves till
               they attain to their abhorr'd ends;
               *All's Well*, Act IV, Scene 3


TIMON.:        … I love my country, and am not one that rejoices in **the
               common wreck**,
               *Timon of Athens*, Act V, Scene 1


PRINCE OF MOROCCO:       Even for that I thank you. Therefore, I
               pray you, lead me to the caskets **to try my fortune**.
               *Merchant of Venice* Act II, Scene 1


PROSPERO.      I'll deliver all;
               And promise you calm seas, **auspicious gales,
               And sail so expeditious** that shall catch
               Your royal fleet far off.
               *The Tempest* Act V, Scene1

In an interview in *The Washington Times*, 4/25/1997, Sir Derek Jacobi said:

I agreed to put my name to a school of thought that maintains that the earl, Edward de Vere, was the author of the plays. Where did this Shakespeare come from? Where did all that knowledge and eloquence and truth come from? ... I am highly suspicious of that gentleman from Stratford on Avon, ... I'm pretty convinced our playwright wasn't that fellow. This opinion is very unpopular with the good burghers of Stratford, I realize, but they also make their living on the legend of Shakespeare's local origins. I don't think it was him.

# PART TWO :

## Curious Clues

# Chapter Five

## Elizabethan Publishing

My interest in the authorship of Shakespeare began in the mid 1980's, when I was teaching history to high school students and started reaching deeper into the Elizabethan era to find interesting term paper topics, beyond the usual Sir Francis Drake or Sir Walter Raleigh. What began as a hobby has become a life-long research project. Once I worked my way through all of the voluminous available material on the Oxford Theory, I was shocked to realize that there were so many intriguing research avenues that had not been yet been explored. Because the entire inertia of Academia has been studiously avoiding all Oxford research vectors, obvious work that needs to be done, with available historical documents, has been left to the hands of volunteer amateurs, and a few motivated free-lance professionals.

I have been reading and researching Elizabethan era books at the New York Public Library since 1993, viewing the original editions on microfilm, and creating my own computer database on the output, unique styles, and literary connections of the most significant printers and publishers of the Elizabethan and Jacobean era in general, but with a specific first focus on the professional output of the men who printed Shakespeare quartos, and those bookmen who are connected to the 17th Earl of Oxford. Because these data are growing in a modern searchable format for the first time, I am beginning to see trends and patterns in Elizabethan publishing that have been obscure up until now.

My principal reference guides include E. Arber's *Transcript of the Registers of the Stationers' Company, 1554-1640*, and Pollard and Redgrave's *A Short-Title Catalog of Books Printed in England, Scotland and Ireland and of English Books Printed abroad (1475-1640)*.

My work is a continuation of the broad surveys begun by R.B. McKerrow, in his *Dictionary of Printers and Booksellers ... 1557-1640* (1913) and his *Printers' and Publishers' Devices in*

*England and Scotland 1485-1640* . I hope to expand on the brilliant framework established by McKerrow, by giving a fuller study of the most significant printers and booksellers in the era of Elizabeth, with attention paid to the literary industry supported by Lords Burghley, Leicester, and Oxford.

Bibliography, especially concerning antique books, has much in common with Archaeology. But paper doesn't hold up as well as stones or bones. We are quite lucky to have any Elizabethan books left intact at all. Because all history, all theory, is based on evidence, we haven't anything close to the whole story, because so much evidence has vanished. So any statements about the number of books assigned to a particular printer, or the number of editions of a certain work, are provisional, and probably wrong. Many of the questions posed by such eminent scholars as W.W. Greg, A.W. Pollard, and R.B. McKerrow have been left unanswered; in part because the important missing links are still missing, but also, because no one has yet had the motivation to look at all the data again, assisted by computers. But that is what I am attempting to begin. The research will have value beyond the particular question of the authorship of Shakespeare. There are other unsolved literary mysteries from the same era. An in-depth effort to collate facts will provide a data pool that may make it possible for other researchers to draw better-informed conclusions. I have been studying the known complete output of several printers, to see what sorts of connections they had; how upturns and downturns in the economy affected what was printed; what was popular, and what was profitable.

Volume 3 of *Pollard & Redgrave* has an index to those Printers and Booksellers actually named on the books and broadsheets, and it provides the STC numbers for the works associated with named tradesmen. For several years now I have been painstakingly looking up all the books listed as numbers in the index for individual printers. There has been no shortcut to this laborious process.

The great scholarship done by Pollard, Gregg, McKerrow, etc. was limited to some degree by the number of texts they had available (in library and museum rare book collections) and could actually look at, and they admittedly missed a lot. Previously "lost" 16th century material has continued to emerge throughout this century. Since the availability of the Short Title collection on microfilm, independent researchers like myself can see every 15th, 16th and 17th Century English book printed, without trudging to London or Washington, and examining one fragile quarto at a time.

## The Stationers' Company

The inner workings of the book publishing industry in the Elizabethan era are fascinating. While booksellers had a longer leash, the printers operated under extraordinary constraints of governmental and guild control. The Stationers' Company was incorporated by royal charter in 1557. The original motivation of the Crown was control of seditious, possibly treasonous books.

One principal function of the Stationers' Company was to censor all printed materials. Originally, all books were read and approved by a panel of high ranking clergy. As the volume of publishing increased it was not possible to read everything prior to printing, so many cases of censorship involved the recall of a book which had been properly licensed, but later, upon closer reading, was found seditious, libelous, or heretical. Fines imposed and collected from individual printers (and sometimes authors) were split 50/50 between the Crown and the Stationers' Company. Interestingly, one category of material that could be printed without censorship was the Greek and Latin Classics.

If a printer died, he could not pass the business on to his son. The inheritance went to the widow. This had two results: printer-widows were highly sought after and could choose their next husband; ones who remained unmarried often printed under their own name. It is a rare and early case of a woman's business status being nearly equal to a man's, in a highly competitive business.

The Stationers' Company was not just an accounting office and trade fraternity, but also a policing force of agents which had remarkable powers of search and seizure. The merest hint or suspicion of illegal books or presses was enough to send in the Wardens. Books, broadsheet ballads, and pamphlets were as highly controlled as illicit substances are today. Punishment for printing illegal books included jail time, huge fines, and sometimes even execution. Despite an abundance of talent and available equipment, a Star Chamber decree of 1586 limited to 25 the number of print shops that were allowed to operate in London. That number stayed fixed for about fifty years. All printing outside of London continued to be prohibited with the exception of one press each at the two Universities, Oxford and Cambridge. Owning a press, or being a licensed user of one, meant being an entered member, a Freeman, of the Stationers' Guild.

Certain printers had Royal patent monopolies allowing them to own the market in a given genre. John Daye had the exclusive on ABC's and Church of England Catechisms. Thomas Marshe held the right to the lucrative monopoly on Latin school books. William Byrd owned the rights to all printed music and even held the copyright on blank music paper. James Roberts had the exclusive on Almanacs and prognostications for several decades. Other printers had no primrose path to profits and had to fend for themselves in the commercial marketplace. It seems to some surprising, but it is this group of desperate printers who turned to ballads and popular plays to keep the presses rolling.

The potential value in this Survey is that it can address the many questions which remain unanswered about why particular authors were printed by individual printers, why everyone kept changing partners and shuffling business around, and what events if any are behind the sale and transfer of valuable copyrights of noted Elizabethan works. Because of the peculiarity of English copyright in the 16th Century, the publishers had all the rights, and the authors had virtually none. Once a work was entered in the Stationers' Register, its copyright was held by the Printer, Bookseller, or Agent who brought in the book and paid the sixpence registration fee. The transfer of copyrights, also registered in the Stationers' Log, are a fascinating thread of inquiry, showing, for instance, how difficult it was for the compilers and publishers of the *First Folio* of Shakespeare to obtain the necessary rights to the plays that had appeared in quarto, some as long as two decades before, and whose ownership had passed through many hands.

## The Shakespeare Canon

The haphazard nature of the first appearances of many of the plays of Shakespeare, with so many different printers involved, has suggested to different historians, different scenarios. Several of the first quartos of Shakespeare have been qualified as "Bad", or "Pirated" or "Misheard " texts. Strangely, none of the so called Shakespeare pirates was ever reprimanded or punished, and in some cases came out with approved Shakespeare texts later.

In the known accepted works of Shakespeare, there are at least 37 different plays in the Canon. Of these 37, at least 19 appeared in quarto editions prior the publication of the *First Folio* of 1623. Of these, orthodox scholarship declares that 13 first editions are "Good Quartos" and 6 are "Bad Quartos". A Good quarto is defined as an early printing of a play wherein the text is nearly identical to later, presumed definitive versions, such as the *First Folio*. A Bad quarto is one in which the text as given is either incomplete, mangled, or substantially different than later, authoritative versions. The prevailing theory is that Bad Quartos were dictated from the memory of actors who had been in the plays, or from partial prompt books. Some modern scholarship, however, has questioned just how "bad" those versions of the plays really are. Several of them seem like deliberately (but poorly) edited shorter versions, based on the scripts of "touring versions" of the plays, which were shorter and called for a smaller number of actors. These plays were later expanded or revised into the form we are familiar with. New thinking on this matter, by  Stratfordian like Eric Sams discounts the entrenched idea of bad quartos.

At this point it is important to clarify what plays and poems are considered to be the standard Shakespeare Canon. The plays are almost entirely defined by the *First Folio* of 1623, which included 36 plays.

Strangely, only 35 plays are named on the *First Folio* contents page, with *Troilus & Cressida* being the odd man out. *Troilus & Cressida* (*T&C*) appears as the first play in the Tragedy section (part III) of the *First Folio*. But the screwed-up page numbering indicates  that it was originally supposed to follow *Romeo & Juliet*, but probably due to several printers being involved and some miscommunication, the play was yanked, then reinserted at the beginning of the section. Standard speculation has to do with the fact that *T&C* was still copyrighted to publishers Bonian and Walley since 1609, and a deal had to be cut. Oxfordian speculation is that the repositioning of *Troilus* (the Truth Teller) adds to its significance. What adds to the strangeness is that the quarto edition of *T&C*, 1609, has a preface that identifies the play as a Comedy.

## These are the 36 Folio Plays as listed, with their 1623 classifications

| | |
|---|---|
| *The Tempest* | Comedy |
| *The Two Gentlemen of Verona* | Comedy |
| *The Merry Wives of Windsor* | Comedy |
| *Measure for Measure* | Comedy |
| *The Comedy of Errors* | Comedy |
| *Much Ado about Nothing* | Comedy |
| *Loves Labours Lost* | Comedy |
| *Midsummer Nights Dreame* | Comedy |
| *The Merchant of Venice* | Comedy |
| *As You Like it* | Comedy |
| *The Taming of the Shrew* | Comedy |
| *All is well that ends well* | Comedy |
| *Twelfe Night, or what you will* | Comedy |
| *The Winters Tale* | Comedy |
| *The Life and Death of King John* | History |
| *The Life and Death of Richard the Second* | History |
| *The First part of King Henry the Fourth* | History |
| *The Second part of King Henry the Fourth* | History |
| *The Life of King Henry the Fifth* | History |
| *The First part of King Henry the Sixth* | History |
| *The Second part of King Henry the Sixth* | History |
| *The Third part of King Henry the Sixth* | History |
| *The Life and Death of Richard the Third* | History |
| *The Life and Death of King Henry the Eighth* | History |
| *The Tragedy of Coriolanus* | Tragedy |
| *Titus Andronicus* | Tragedy |
| *Romeo and Juliet* | Tragedy |
| *Timon of Athens* | Tragedy |
| *The Life and Death of Julius Caesar* | Tragedy |
| *The Tragedy of Macbeth* | Tragedy |
| *The Tragedy of Hamlet* | Tragedy |
| *King Lear* | Tragedy |
| *Othello the Moor of Venice* | Tragedy |
| *Anthony and Cleopatra* | Tragedy |
| *Cymbeline King of Britaine* | Tragedy |
| *Troilus & Cressida* | |

*Pericles, Prince of Tyre*, which is missing from the *First Folio*, is generally considered to be the 37$^{th}$ Canon play. After this are the semi-acceptable Apocryphal Plays:

*The Two Noble Kinsmen*
*Sir Thomas More*
*Famous Victories of Henry 5*
*Edward III*

## The accepted poetry :

*Venus & Adonis*
*Rape of Lucrece*
*Phoenix and the Turtle*
*Sonnets*
*A Lovers Complaint*

# Chapter Six

# The Shakespeare Quartos and Their Printers

Orthodox scholarship holds that Shaksper-of-Stratford had nothing at all to do with the publication of the plays in quarto. The plays are assumed to have been the exclusive property of the Lord Chamberlains Men, or the King's Men, or other theatrical companies. The orthodox theory is that after individual plays were no longer popular on the stage, copies would be allowed to "escape" to perhaps make a little extra money by collaborating with a printer or bookseller. Plague closed the theaters for several seasons in the 1590's, and some scholars have posited that the theater companies allowed their precious plays to be printed only out of desperation. Standard scholars rarely address the question of why Shaksper-of-Stratford didn't try to cash in on the 16 to 18 plays that remained unprinted during his lifetime, and only were published seven years after his death, in the *First Folio*, 1623. The standard theorists are forced to "conclude" that the *Folio* group of plays were in the possession of the Kings Men, but for some reason the majority were never performed, or no record of such performance survives. Oxfordian theory suggests that the *Folio* plays package, held in trust by the Herbert brothers, the Earls of Pembroke, and Montgomery, were the dramas written by Edward de Vere in the 1570's and 1580's and performed only at Court. For Oxford, there was no need to print plays to make money, so that the plays that did see print, particularly the "good" quartos, must have been permitted by de Vere, seeing some social or political value in having his message read. So the plays held back from printing were probably withheld on purpose. If, in fact, Edward de Vere authored the plays, he and his heirs would have had many reasons for concealing his involvement. Perhaps the de Vere family was waiting for a new political climate to emerge in England, one in which it would be possible to publish the Works under the author's true name. That climate never emerged, and with the rise of the power of the Puritans and the looming English Civil

War, the publication of the plays in Folio in 1623 may have been a "now or never" compromise.

The bulk of the "Shakespeare" first issues occurred during the last decade of Oxford's life. Sixteen different Canon plays came out in Quarto from 1594 - 1604. Nine are classed as "good", seven as "bad". But two plays, *Romeo & Juliet*, and *Hamlet*, received updates and appeared in full text 2nd Printings, also in Vere's lifetime. So all told there were at least 11 Good, or full text plays printed and frequently reprinted in this same time frame. If Vere wrote the original works, he must have at least *agreed* to the printing of some of the good quartos. My reasoning is this : the copies of these quartos still exist, they were never banned and burned carte-blanche (as was ordered for the works of Nashe and Harvey). Most of the Quarto plays received official entries in the Stationers' Register. The printers who printed the plays were not arrested, nor did they suddenly go out of business. Oxford was a Peer of the Realm at the top of the aristocratic social hierarchy, and a senior member of the House of Lords. He received a yearly Government grant of a thousand pounds, for unspecified service to Queen and country. If he had been displeased about these books appearing he could have immediately quashed the phenomena. I'm not suggesting that Oxford was actively supervising the publication of all the Quartos. A few of the quartos were almost certainly "pirated". But there are a few items where Oxfords participation can be argued : The "good" Q2 of *Romeo and Juliet*, *Midsummer Nights Dream*, Q1, and the "good" *Hamlet*, Q2. But even if many of the quartos were printed without Oxford's direct permission or participation, the printers themselves seem to have left clues that point to his authorship.

The first smoking gun in the Shakespeare Problem is the phenomenon of the held back plays. Keep in mind the 36 Folio Plays that were published together in 1623. Only half were printed during the lifetime of Shaksper-of-Stratford. The rest were held in trust (we presume). The list follows:

## First Edition "Shakespeare" Plays that appeared in Quarto before 1623

| | | | |
|---|---|---|---|
| *Titus Andronicus* | Q1 | 1594 | "Good" |
| Henry the Sixth, Part 2 *"First Part of the Contention"* | Q1 | 1594 | "Bad" |
| Henry the Sixth Part 3 *"True Tragedie of Richard..."* | Q1 | 1595 | "Bad" |
| *The Tragedie of King Richard the Second* | Q1 | 1597 | "Good" |
| *The Tragedie of King Richard the Third* | Q1 | 1597 | "Good" |
| *Romeo and Juliet* | Q1 | 1597 | "Bad" |
| *Loves Labors Lost* | Q1 | 1598 | "Good |
| *The History of Henry the Fourth* (H4 P1) | Q1 | 1598 | "Good" |
| *Much Ado about Nothing* | Q1 | 1600 | "Good" |
| *A Midsummer Nights Dreame* | Q1 | 1600 | "Good" |
| *The Merchant of Venice* | Q1 | 1600 | "Good" |
| *The Second part of Henry the Fourth* | Q1 | 1600 | "Good" |
| *The Chronicle History of Henry the Fifth* | Q1 | 1600 | "Bad" |
| *The Merry Wives of Windsor* | Q1 | 1602 | "Bad" |
| *The Tragicall Historie of Hamlet* | Q1 | 1603 | "Bad" |
| *King Lear* | Q1 | 1608 | "Bad" |
| *Troilus & Cressida* | Q1 | 1609 | "Good" |
| *Othello the Moor of Venice* | Q1 | 1622 | "Good" |

## Held-back Shakespeare Plays first printed in the *Folio* of 1623

*The Tempest*
*The Two Gentlemen of Verona*
*Measure for Measure*
*The Comedy of Errors*
*As You Like it*
*The Taming of the Shrew*
*All is well that ends well*
*Twelfe Night, or what you will*
*The Winters Tale*
*The Life and Death of King John*
*The First part of King Henry the Sixth*
*The Life and Death of King Henry the Eighth*
*The Tragedy of Coriolanus*
*Timon of Athens*
*The Life and Death of Julius Caesar*
*The Tragedy of Macbeth*
*Anthony and Cleopatra*
*Cymbeline King of Britaine*

This final group of 18 plays, including comedies and tragedies for which Shakespeare is so famous, were never printed in "Shakespeare's" day. Many of them were never even performed. How can this be ?   Shakespeare the playwright is supposed to have hit his peak of artistry and theatrical success during the 1605 to 1616 era. Yet there is scant record of new Shakespeare plays being popular or regularly performed for the paying public at that time. Shaksper the man was in business in the country and can not be connected to the Jacobean London activities imagined for him in retrospect by desperate biographers. The 18 held-back Shakespeare plays, that emerged from oblivion in 1623, but had never been printed in the author's lifetime, are a problem for the standard biographers of Shakespeare.

The notion that William Shaksper could have resisted selling or profiting from these properties, if he really had them, is incompatible with the record of his petty lawsuits and lust for payment. So the standard story is that Shaksper had no access to these plays. Why the King's Men or other alleged theatrical owners didn't sell any of the 18 scripts to printers in lean times, if *they* really owned them, is an unanswered mystery.

Many of the Shakespeare plays that are assumed to have been popular in the Jacobean age were demonstrably not.

*Timon of Athens* has no performance history until 1678.
*Coriolanus* has no stage history until 1682.
*King John*, although mentioned by Meres in 1598 has no stage history until 1737.

Perhaps most shocking are the first performance dates for three of the most well known plays in the Canon:

*All's Well That Ends Well* in 1741;
*Anthony and Cleopatra* in 1759; and

*Two Gentlemen of Verona,* not known to have been played until 1762.

*Troilus & Cressida* is more complicated. It was printed in 1609 in two variant editions. Version One claims that the play had been performed by the King's Men at the Globe. Version Two, which contains the preface "A never writer , to an ever reader.   Newes.", claims that the play is brand new and was "never staled with the Stage,  never clapper-clawed with the palmes of the vulger." The first documented performance of Troilus wasn't until 1679.

How does the standard model address the non performance of these and other so-called "Late Plays", given the chronology they use for the play's composition and the premise that Shakespeare wrote for money, and to order?  In the Oxford scenario, these "lost plays" were Court productions from the 1580's and 90's that Oxford entertained Queen Elizabeth with. They are not picked up by Stratfordian radar, because they are looking for performances in the wrong era.

## The Earl of Oxford and the Printers

The 17th Earl of Oxford can be linked to key Elizabethan publishers and printers for over four decades. It began with his relationship with William Seres. Seres was a big shot in publishing, from the earliest days of Elizabeth until about 1578. He was the original printer of the Golding (Vere) version of *Ovid's Metamorphoses*, in its first (1565) and fully developed versions (1567 and 1575). But there is also that famous record of payment from Oxford's youth (when he was Cecil's ward) which includes a large purchase from Mr. Seres, including, almost certainly, the very Geneva Bible, annotated by Oxford, that survives at the Folger. The famous pay-entry reads:

To William Seres, stationer, for a Geneva Bible, gilt, a Chaucer, Plutarch's works in French, with other books and papers ...

There are dozens of important books from his era that praise Oxford for his patronage of literature in general, and for encouraging the creation and publication of the work in question. The Earl of Oxford was one of several major patrons of literature in his day.

In terms of sheer numbers both William Cecil and the Earl of Leicester were honored by, or patronized more books. But "Oxford's Books", have a robust, hyper-intelligent and even bawdy character, a special collection in publishing history because they can be shown to be the reading matter and the linguistic universe that "Shake-speare", as poet and wordsmith resided in.

The Oxford related Books, including : *The Courtier* in Latin, 1571; *Cardanus Comfort*, 1573; *The New Jewel of Health*, 1576; *Zelauto*, 1580; *Hekatompathia*, 1582; *Euphues and his England*, 1580; *The English Secretary*,1586 are all pivotal pieces of the literary Renaissance in England, and these books are found reflected in the themes and language of the Shakespeare plays. *Cardanus Comfort* is the book Hamlet is holding and quoting from when he gives his "To be or not ..." speech. *Hekatompathia* is a source for *Othello*. *Zelauto* inspired plot elements of the *Merchant of Venice*.

In Stephen Booth's edition of *Shakespeare's Sonnets*, take a look at pages 398 and 399. Here Booth displays the title page of *The New Jewel of Health*, 1576. Booth relates the alchemical equipment in the drawing to Sonnet 119, which uses an extended alchemical metaphor, naming devices and methods described in the *New Jewell*. What Booth never mentions is that the author, George Baker, was family doctor to Edward de Vere, and that the book has both a lavish dedication to Oxford's wife the countess Anne, and a full page depiction of the Vere Arms and motto: Vero Nihil Verius. The book was an expensive production, with many made-to-order woodcut illustrations. In plain language, a book that Stratfordians think "may have inspired Shakespeare", turns out to have emerged from Oxford's household, at a time when the Stratford man was only 12 years old. It is much more likely that this alchemy book inspired the author of the Shakespeare plays because it was his own project.

¶ The newe Iewell of Health, wherein is contayned the most excellent Secretes of Phisicke and Philosophie, deuided into fower Bookes. In the which are the best approued remedies for the diseases as well inwarde as outwarde, of all the partes of mans bodie : treating very amplye of all Distillations of Waters, of Oyles, Balmes, Quintessences, with the extraction of artificiall Saltes, the vse and preparation of Antimonie, and potable Gold. Gathered out of the best and most approued Authors, by that excellent Doctor Gesnerus. Also the Pictures, and maner to make the Vessels, Furnaces, and other Instrumentes therevnto belonging. Faithfully corrected and published in Englishe, by George Baker, Chirurgian.

ALCHYMYA

Printed at London, by Henrie Denham.
1 5 7 6.

¶To the Right Honourable, Vertuous, and his singular good Lady, the Noble Countesse of Oxeforde. &c. your humble seruaunt wisheth long lyfe, prosperous health, and dayly encrease of Honour.

T IS VVRITTEN (RIGHT Honourable and my singular good Lady) that Philip King of Macedonia reioyced greatly when his sonne Alexander vvas borne, bicause his Empyre shoulde not lacke a gouernour after his death, but herein he reioyced much more, that his sonne vvas borne in the time of Aristotle that learned Philosopher, by whome he vvas taught and instructed ten yeares. And in lyke maner it fareth novv vvith me, as vvith the King of Macedonia, and no lesse is my ioye; than the delight of that mightie Prince. Herein I doe reioyce, that this vvorke of Distillation is novve finished to the profite of my countrie, vvherein great studie and long labour hath bene earnestly bestovved. But I reioyce much more that it is finished in the time of you my Honourable, vertuous, and good Ladie, to vvhose learned vevue and fauourable protection I offer this Booke, as a due testimonie of my seruiceable heart, and as some fruites of my poore paynfull studie and practise, vvishing that it vvere in value counternayleable to the condigne demerites of your so Honourable expectation, so as euery lyne, in respect of my loyaltie, might supplye a nevve Iewell for your Nevve yeares gift, albeit, you haue no neede of Golde and Ievvels, abounding honourably in all riches : Notvvithstanding, this booke maye be truely termed the nevve Iewell of health, vvhich before this daye vvas neuer seene or published abroade by anye other man. This nevve Iewell vvyll make the blynde to see, and the lame to vvalke. This nevv Iewell
A ij.                                    vvill

*New Jewell of Health*, title page (left) and dedication (right).

Oxford's name, and talent, were either on display, or being praised by name overtly, in over 80 books while he was alive (including reprints and revised editions.) The names Henry Bynneman, Thomas Marshe, and Thomas East, John Allde, Gabriel Cawood, John Wolfe, John Charlewood, Robert Waldegrave, William Ponsonby, Richard Jones, William Wright, , Abel Jeffes, Thomas Orwin, Thomas Creede, Richard Field, Cuthbert Burby, Peter Short, James Roberts, Simon Stafford, Edward White, John Danter, John Harrison, and many others are associated with Oxford publications.

From the list above, take note of the last nine. For Creede, Field, Burby, Short, Roberts, Stafford, White, Danter, Harrison, were all printers or sellers of Shakespeare Quartos.

These printers and sellers, who are linked both to Oxford-patronized books and to some of the Shakespeare texts, also turn out to be key suppliers of works classified as Shakespeare apocrypha, as well as works that Shakespeare drew upon, the so called "Sources of Shakespeare", which include everything from Holinshed's chronicles, to translations, anonymous plays, poetry, and editions of the Psalms.

## Shakespeare and the Printers

The standard story about Shakespeare the playwright is that he had no monetary or commercial rights to his plays once they had been purchased by a theatrical company. The theaters or acting companies owned the plays, and would only sell a manuscript to a printer after the play had lost its box office appeal. In seasons where the theaters were shut by plague or by city edict, a larger number of popular plays were printed, as a way of generating income from these "properties", which at the time could be capitalized on in no other way.

Because there is nothing in the way of a historical paper trail to connect the William Shaksper of Stratford-on-Avon to the printers of the Shakespeare plays, historians have had to completely invent, through conjecture and extrapolation, what happened in the case of Shakespeare's plays. *The Reader's Encyclopedia of Shakespeare* sums up the problem from the conventional view: "Once sold, the rights to a play belonged in perpetuity to the printer, even if the play had been sold without the author's knowledge or consent. Without an author's supervision of the printing, the correction of errors, or the initiation of necessary changes, texts suffered corruption in the publication process."

Does having the script of a play available to the public really make that play any less appealing to be witnessed live in the theater? The orthodox explanation is that theater owners were worried that rival companies or college amateurs would perform their play due to available scripts. But this dismisses the fact that amateur and/or bad productions of *Hamlet* don't prevent people from going to see the play, properly performed by professionals. And many of the attendees to Elizabethan theater were illiterate anyway, so having the play published should really have had no effect on attendance. It is, in general, true that the printing of plays in the Elizabethan era usually followed a theatrical run of the drama. In many cases, however, the only evidence of the theatrical history are the statements on the printed Quartos themselves, such as: "... performed by Her Majesties Servants ...". The publishers of 400 years ago knew the same marketing tie-in tricks that are the stock in trade today.

In the case of the Shakespeare Quartos published prior to 1623, there were 19 individual "accepted" plays, and 3 works of poetry, which adds up to 22 separate Shakespeare works. These works were reprinted and often modified or updated in a variety of editions. Counting up all the original and reprint editions of these works from 1593 to 1623, I found that there were no less than 73 individual publications of Shakespeare texts over those three decades. Of the 73 editions, 39 appeared from 1593 to 1604; another 21 from 1605 to 1616; and 13 more from 1617 to 1623.

In terms of First Quartos, or just the original appearances of the plays:

| Era: | First Quartos | Reprints | Accepted "Shakespeare" books |
|---|---|---|---|
| 1593 -1604 | 17 | 22 | 39 |
| 1605 -1616 | 4 | 17 | 21 |
| 1617 -1623 | 1 | 12 | 13 |
| Totals | 22 works | | 73 publications |

The story on each book is so different that the facts hardly fit the scenario presented by the standard Stratfordian explanation. Shakespeare the playwright is supposed (in the standard story) to have hit his peak of artistry and theatrical success during the 1605 to 1616 era. Yet there is scant record of new Shakespeare plays being popular or regularly performed at that time. Shaksper the man was in business in the country and can not be connected to the activities imagined for him in retrospect by desperate biographers. And there is the awful matter of the 18 other Shakespeare plays, that emerged from oblivion in 1623, but were never printed in the author's lifetime. How Shaksper could have resisted selling these properties is incompatible with the record of his petty lawsuits, and lust for payment. So the standard story is that he had no access to these plays, and why the Kings Men or other alleged owners didn't sell scripts to printers in lean times is an unanswered mystery. But the facts speak for themselves.

After 1604, access to authentic Shakespeare material dried up.

And there is no reason to believe that the post 1604 texts were written post 1604. *Troilus & Cressida*, which was first printed in 1609, and is often held up as proof that Shakespeare was still writing at that date, was actually entered in the Stationers' Register on Feb. 7, 1603.

The orthodox accepted works of "Shakespeare" include at least 37 Plays in the canon. Of these 37, 19 appeared in Quarto editions prior the publication of the *First Folio* of 1623. Of the first editions of these 19 plays, orthodox scholarship declares that 13 items are "Good Quartos" and 6 are "Bad Quartos". A Good quarto is defined as an early printing of a play wherein the text is nearly identical to later, presumed definitive versions, such as the *First Folio*. A Bad quarto is one in which the text as given is either incomplete, mangled, or substantially different from later, authoritative versions. The prevailing theory is that Bad Quartos were dictated from the memory of actors who had been in the plays, or from partial prompt books. A reasonable counter-theory is that several of the early "bad" quartos were printed from the scripts of early "touring versions" of the plays, which were shorter and called for a smaller number of actors.

# Chapter Seven

## Shakespeare as Editor

### Why did Shakespeare stop editing books in 1604?

The orthodox position on Shakespeare's relationship to the publishers of his plays is that he had virtually none. In the course of looking at all these publications on microfilm, and assembling a database of information about the books, I have come across some peculiar facts that alone seem innocent, but assembled together, point a reasoning mind to the conclusion that the standard view of the Shakespeare publications is completely in error. The author did interact with the publishers, and in a powerful way, at least on several occasions.

In the many individual Shakespeare Quartos that appeared from 1593 to 1622 (at least 73 different editions) there are only a small number, (5), that indicate on the title page that the text had been altered, improved or enlarged, with the statement or the suggestion that the changes were made by the author. Because the author was not supposed to be involved in the quarto publications, the academic spin is that the announcement of corrections and additions by the author were a marketing gimmick coming from the commercial mind of the publisher. But these are not modest corrections, that any copyist could accomplish. We are talking about the complete authentic texts of *Romeo & Juliet* and *Hamlet* for instance.

Following the existing paper trail, "Shake-speare" can be shown to have edited some of his own books, for improved published editions, from only 1598 to 1604. After 1604, access to texts and to the original editor was permanently interrupted. The remarkable thing is that these five instances of advertised authorial corrections and additions all occurred during the time span of 1598 – 1604.

In other words, there was a short window of time, six years, that "Shakespeare the author" showed an active involvement in improving printed versions of his works, long after the plays had been popular on stage originally. After 1604, Shakespeare was apparently unavailable for revisions.

The Quartos that "Shakespeare" edited (or so it says on the title pages):

| Play | Quarto | Year | Printed by | For |
|------|--------|------|------------|-----|
| *Loves Labours Lost* | Q1 | 1598 | William White | Cuthbert Burby |
| *Henry the 4th Part 1* | Q2 | 1599 | Simon Stafford | Andrew Wise |
| *Romeo & Juliet* | Q2 | 1599 | Thomas Creede | Cuthbert Burby |
| *Richard III* | Q3 | 1602 | Thomas Creede | Andrew Wise |
| *Hamlet* | Q2 | 1604 | James Roberts | Nicholas Ling |

## Loves Labors Lost

In this group of quartos that claim authorial revision, *Loves Labors Lost* is the only first edition in the bunch, and precisely because of the claim of emendation, scholars do believe that there was probably an earlier edition of *Loves Labors Lost*. If there is a lost edition of "*Lost*", then this so-called Q1 is actually a Q2. *LLL* was also the first printed play to actually name "W. Shakespere." The printer was William White and the publisher was Cuthbert Burby. The exact wording of the title page is as follows:

> A Pleasant Conceited Comedie called Loves labors lost.
> As it was presented before her Highnes this last Christmas.
> Newly corrected and augmented
>  By W. Shakespere.
> Imprinted at London by W.W. for Cutbert Burby. 1598.

*A*

# PLEASANT

## Conceited Comedie
### CALLED,
## Loues labors loſt.

As it vvas preſented before her Highnes
this laſt Chriſtmas.

Newly correcked and augmented
*By W. Shakeſpere.*

Imprinted at London by *W.W.*
for *Cutbert Burby.*
1598.

No entry in the Stationers' Register matches the 1598 printing. The work first appears in the SR in 1607 when Ling (the publisher of *Hamlet*) entered his copy to establish rights, with a notation that both a Court and Burby had provided written permission. Ling in fact acquired three interesting texts from Burby in 1607: *LLL*, *Romeo & Juliet*, and *Taming of A Shrew*, (the apocryphal version of *Taming of the Shrew*). But Ling did not print *LLL* in 1607. Instead he died that year, and his newly acquired Shakespeare properties were transferred to John Smethwicke, whose ownership won him a place as one of the printers of the *First Folio* and the *Second Folio*.

It is not possible to verify that *LLL* was played for the Queen at Christmas of 1597, as implied by the title page. The advertisement is the sole evidence. If there was an earlier publication of *LLL* before the enigmatic 1598 printing, perhaps the performance for the Queen might have been at an earlier Christmas. One standard scholar (Wilson) dated the original performance of *LLL* as a 1593 private performance for the Earl of Southampton. This is still an open question. But *Loves Labors Lost* has no history on the public stage whatsoever, until 1839. It was not a hit play or something that people had seen, when the 1598 text went on sale. In the standard paradigm of authorship it is very hard to explain how Shaksper of Stratford, who had retired to the country, was induced to re-write, expand or revise this play for publication, when it had no particular market, and Shakespeare's name had never even appeared on a play before. Interestingly, Cuthbert Burby, in 1598 also published *Palladis Tamia*, the book that in one breath praises the Earl of Oxford as the best of the comic dramatists, and in another whisper, launches the name "Shakespeare", assigning this virtual unknown a large body of works including *Loves Labors Lost* and the mysterious *"Love's Labors Won."*

Now here is an interesting piece of the puzzle that has never emerged until my research.

Cuthbert Burby was not a printer. He was a bookseller of note. He didn't just have a stall in the courtyard; he had his own shop at the Royal Exchange.

In 1595, Cuthbert Burby obtained the rights to *The English Secretary* by Angel Daye, a work originally published in 1586, with a lavish dedication to the Earl of Oxford and a full page block print of the Vere coat of Arms in its most complex form with Harpy, blue boar and surmounted by a falcon. Burby published a reprint of the original work in 1595 (the Q3), but then apparently commissioned Angel Daye to revise and expand the book, because in 1599, *The English Secretary* was published by Burby in an all new, expanded edition, featuring a new dedication to the Earl of Oxford. That dedication begins : "To the right Honorable , Edward de Vere, Earle of Oxenford, Vicount Bulbecke, Lord Standford and of Badlesmere, and Lord great Chamberlaine of England. It is now a few years past (Right Honourable, & my very good Lord) since emboldened by your favour, this booke rudely digested, and then roughly delivered, I did in the very nonage thereof recommend unto your patronage..." It is not unlikely that some Oxford money passed into the hands of Burby and Daye in 1599. In addition to *Palladis Tamia*, which mentions Oxford, and *The English Secretary*, Burby published a third work with an overt de Vere connection. The book was *Axiochus*, credited bizarrely to "Edw. Spenser" in 1592. The printers were John Danter and John Charlewood and the publisher was Cuthbert Burby. The title page says : " Heereto is annexed a sweet speech or Oration, spoken at the triumphe at White-Hall before her Majestie, by the page to the right noble Earle of Oxenforde. " This speech actually dates from a Tournament in the 1580's.

The 1598 publication of *Loves Labors Lost,* which boasts revisions by Shakespeare, cannot be adequately explained using the standard framework, as the Stratford man was in the country, and the play was not currently popular, on stage or on the printed page. But the publisher of the book was Cuthbert Burby, who can be easily linked to the Earl of Oxford in publishing projects of the same time period. Burby also had access to a number of Anonymous plays, some which ended up in the Shakespeare Apocrypha such as *Taming of A Shrew*, 1594, and some which were attributed to Robert Greene: *George a Greene the Pinner of Wakefield*, and *Orlando Furioso* for examples.

## Henry the Fourth, Part 1, Q2

The Q1 of *Henry IV part 1* had been printed by Peter Short for Andrew Wise in 1598. It was duly registered that year, on Feb. 25, 1598. That first quarto is Anonymous. There is nothing about it that identifies the work as related to Shakespeare.

Wise, in his second edition, printed by Simon Stafford in 1599, assigned the play to the mysterious new playwright, Shake-speare. *Henry the Fourth, Part 1* Q2, of 1599, is considered a "Good Quarto" containing the complete text.

The Title Page says :

> The History of Henrie the Fourth;
> With the batell at Shrewsburie, betweene the King and Lord Henry Percy, surnamed Henry Hotspur of the North. With the humorous conceits of Sir John Falstaffe.
> Newly corrected by W. Shake-speare. Printed by S. S. for Andrew Wise ... 1599

The Q2, or "Shakespeare corrected text" is really not that different from the Q1. Standard scholars do not conjecture that the publisher Wise contacted Shakespeare for a rewrite. The peculiar statement : " Newly corrected by W. Shake-speare. " is generally not commented on.

But here is a peculiarity. The 1598 publication by Meres, *Palladis Tamia*, credited Shakespeare for the first time with 12 plays, listed here with his unique spellings and titles: *Gentlemen of Verona, Errors, Love labors lost , Love labours wonne, Midsummers night dreame, Merchant of Venice, Richard II, Richard III, Henry IV, King John, Titus Andronicus,* and *Romeo & Juliet.*

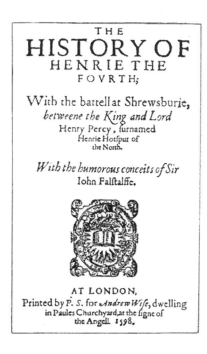
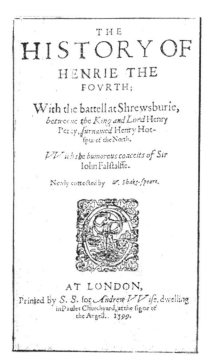

**Henry IV Part 1 title pages.** Left: First Quarto, Anonymous, 1598. Right: Second Quarto, "Newly corrected", 1599.

But in 1598, only 6 of those named works ( *Titus Andronicus,* *Richard II, Richard III, Love Labors Lost, Romeo & Juliet,* and *Henry IV*) had been printed. *Two Gentlemen of Verona, The* *Comedy of Errors,* and *King John* were never printed until 1623. *Titus, Richard II, Richard III,* and *Henry IV part 1* all appeared anonymously in their first editions. So the author of the list used by Meres (presumably F. Meres himself) had access to a certain amount of information that had no verifiable counterpart in the real world.

*Henry IV part 1* came out anonymously by Wise in February 1598. *Palladis Tamia* wasn't registered until September 1598, and presumably appeared in bookstores that fall. Wise, in his second edition of 1599 assigned the play to the unknown

"Shake-speare". Why ? Perhaps to conform to the new "rules" regarding Shakespeare, or to simply capitalize on his name.

## Simon Stafford

Let us now consider the team that brought out the Q2 of *Henry the Fourth, Part 1*, the printer Simon Stafford, and the publisher Andrew Wise. Simon Stafford is an extremely interesting fellow. Born around 1561, he was an apprentice in the Drapers Company to the famous Christopher Barker. Barker had managed to abandon draping for printing; he achieved a rare full transfer to the Stationers' Guild, and he became the Queen's printer. So Simon Stafford, who was a relative of Sir Edward Stafford, was a student in one of the busiest and best financed print shops in London.

Like his master, Stafford wished to become a printer in his own right, and after he earned his freedom within the Drapers he continued to do printing work. In 1597, Stafford obtained an almost inexplicable grant from the Archbishop of Canterbury, including funds from the legacy or Sir Richard Champion. Stafford bought a printing press, applied for a permit from the Stationers, and began printing without waiting for approval. Because Stafford was a freeman of the Drapers guild, the Stationers refused. The full story gets very complicated, but on March 13, 1598, Stafford was raided in his home by a team of Wardens of the Stationers' Company led by none other than Cuthbert Burby. Stafford's press, type, stock of paper and books were all confiscated, and he was prohibited from further printing. Amazingly, because of Stafford's incredible connections in the aristocracy, he was granted appeal after appeal, and after several months of legal maneuverings and court appearances, Stafford was granted, on Sept. 10, 1598, the right to print and admittance into the Stationers' Company.

The document granting Stafford his rights begins:

The copie of the Counsells order sett downe touchinge Stafford - 10 Sept. 1598 Sonday - At the Court at Greenwiche the 10 of September present:

| | |
|---|---|
| Lord Keeper | (Thomas **Egerton**) |
| Lord Admiral | (Charles **Howard**) |
| Lord Chamberlain | ( **Oxford** ? ) |
| Lord North | ( Roger Lord North) |
| Lord Buckhurst | (Thomas **Sackville**) |
| Master Comptroler | (Sir William Knollys) |
| Master Secretary | ( Robert Cecil ? ) |
| Sir John **Fortescue** | (Chancellor of the Exchequer) |

That's a rather high power bunch deciding what would normally be a minor guild affair, settled out of court. Stafford had powerful friends. The next question is: which person is indicated on the above list by the appellation "Lord Chamberlain" ? In 1598 Edward de Vere was Lord Great Chamberlain of England, and George Carey, Lord Hunsdon was the Lord Chamberlain of the Queens Household.

As in other official documents, the signatures are penned in order of rank and custom. Oxford, as Lord Great Chamberlain, put his signature usually 3$^{rd}$ or 4$^{th}$ depending on who else was present who might have "outranked" him, by civil formula, at that moment.

A document dated April 1603, which authorizes the funding for the transportation of the new King James from Scotland to London, is signed by most of the surviving Noblemen of Elizabeth's Court.
The first 5 signatures are:

John Whitgift, Archbishop of Canterbury
Sir Thomas **Egerton**, Lord Chancellor & Lord Keeper
Sir Thomas **Sackville**, Lord Buckhurst
Edward de Vere, 17th Earl of **Oxford**
Charles **Howard**, 10th Earl of Nottingham

It is not impossible, due the order of precedence of the signatures, and the similarity to other signed documents, that the Earl of Oxford was present during the Simon Stafford hearing.

A further fascinating Oxfordian connection to this is that Simon Stafford was the printer and publisher of the peculiar publication *Anagrammata* which appeared in 1603.

*Anagrammata* honors thirteen leading noblemen of the time including Oxford. The 13 men were:

Lord Keeper Thomas **Egerton**
Admiral Charles **Howard**, Earl of Nottingham
Thomas **Sackville**, Lord Buckhurst
Charles Blount (Lord Mountjoy)
John **Fortescue**
Gilbert Talbot, Earl of Shrewsbury
Henry Percy, Earl of Northumberland
Edward de Vere, Earl of **Oxford**
Henry Wriothesley, Earl of Southampton
John Stanhope
Sir Julius Caesar
George Carey, L. C. of the Household
John Swinnerton (Sherrif of London)

It is fascinating that five of the men honored in this publication were on the high commission which granted Stafford his full rights and caused him to be finally admitted as a freeman of the Stationers' Guild. And the juxtaposition of Oxford and Southampton, in the company of Sir Julius Caesar, brings us into the heart of Shakespeare country.

The passage in *Anagrammata* on the Earl of Oxford reads, in Latin:

EDOUARDUS VEIERUS  per Anagramma  AURE SURDUS VIDEO

    Auribus hisce licet studio, fortuna, susurros
    Perfidiae, et technas efficis esse procul,
    At tamen accipio, quae mens horrescit, et auris,
    Rebus facta malis corpore surda tenus,
    Imo etiam cerno Catilinae fraude propinquos
    Funere solventes fata aliena suo.

What follows is a new translation, by me, guided and informed by previous work by Andy Hannas and Alex Watts-Tobin:

Edovardus Veierus   by anagram:  **Aure Surdus Video**
"**Though Deaf in Ear, I see**"

With these ears, by Fortune, in study I remain
far from treachery and whisperings.
Yet nevertheless, I take in those things

at which both the mind and ears must shudder.
Those deeds, bent on evil, are deaf to my body.
And more, I even see kinsmen, with the deceit of Catiline
paying for fate severely with their own death.

The reference to Catiline is instructive. Catiline (108 B.C. - 62 B.C.) was a Roman politician, and is notorious for having led a disastrous conspiracy against the dictatorship of Sulla. Though the two men had been friends, Sulla's corrupt regime and the resulting economic dispossession of many leading Romans fomented a treacherous reaction. Cicero, the Consul of Rome under Sulla, discovered the Catiliniarian conspiracy, and all of the participants, including Catiline, were executed. As this passage in *Anagrammata* appeared in 1603, the timing is too early to refer to the famous Gunpowder Plot of 1604-5. My take on this is that the disastrous Essex conspiracy and attempted coup d'etat of 1601 is the event alluded to here. Robert Cecil played the role that Cicero had created 17 centuries earlier. There is even a similarity in the names of the investigators. Cecil / Cicero.

Because of title and theme of this poem, involving Deafness, some Oxford scholars are considering the possibility that Edward de Vere became deaf in the final years of his life.

Here follow a few examples from Shakespeare, who repeats the theme of deafness, both physical and "attitudinal", throughout the works.

Though now this grained face of mine be hid
In sap-consuming winter's drizzled snow,
And all the conduits of my blood froze up,
Yet hath my night of life some memory,
My wasting lamps some fading glimmer left,
My dull deaf ears a little use to hear;
    *Comedy of Errors*, Act V, Scene 1


Such men as he be never at heart's ease
Whiles they behold a greater than themselves,
And therefore are they very dangerous.
I rather tell thee what is to be fear'd
Than what I fear, for always I am Caesar.

89

Come on my right hand, for this ear is deaf,
And tell me truly what thou think'st of him.
*Julius Caesar*, Act I, Scene 2

When in disgrace with Fortune and men's eyes,
I all alone beweep my outcast state,
And trouble deaf heaven with my bootless cries,
And look upon my self and curse my fate,
*Sonnet 29*

The work *Anagrammata* is entirely in Latin and the notation at the bottom says:

HONORIS ERGO
AB      A. L. S.
F. D.
Londini, ex officina Simonis Stafford.
  1603

which translates as:

On Account of Honor
By A. L S.
In London, from the workshop (or office) of Simon Stafford.   1603

The phrase "from the workshop of" is extremely rare in publishing of this era.

An incredible fact never addressed by the standard commentators is the 'about face' of Cuthbert Burby, who originally initiated the lawsuit against Stafford and personally led the high handed raid confiscating Stafford's gear. Immediately after the high court ruled in Stafford's favor, Burby hired Stafford to do the printing on several interesting works. Stafford and Burby issued *George a Greene the Pinner of Wakefield* 1599. The two men also brought out the second edition of *King Edward the Third* in 1599. This anonymous play is only now gaining acceptance as a true Shakespeare play, 400 years after the fact.

Simon Stafford also printed *Summers Last will and Testament* 1600 . This work is very Vere oriented, and is under massive investigation right now by myself and others for significant leads.

Stafford also printed the apocryphal *King Leir* 1605 and the Q2 of *Pericles* in 1611. It is my hypothesis at this point that Oxford knew Stafford and pulled some strings for him. Stafford, as a "made man" in the Guild, was then a trusted conduit for sensitive manuscripts.

Stafford somehow obtained the emblems and equipment of John Danter, who was a fascinating rogue and part time "Shakespeare Pirate Publisher". Danter, ironically, gets credit for printing the very first (though Anonymous) Shakespeare play : *Titus Andronicus* of 1594. Danter also printed a revival of *The15 books of Ovid' Metamorphosis* by Golding (Vere). Danter endured a major Star Chamber ordeal in 1597 as a result of printing a Catholic book, the *Jesus Psalter*.

Somehow, even though he had his equipment taken, Danter printed the incredibly botched first quarto of *Romeo & Juliet* in 1597. His career had spanned a decade and he had printed dozens of books. *R&J* was practically his last. Danter's name appears on only 3 books after *R&J* and the "story" is that he died in either 1598 or 1599. But there is no tidy end to the story, no official transfers of property, as often happens in the print trade. All we have is the evidence of the typefaces and emblems, and it is clear that around 1599, Simon Stafford came into the possession of Danter's emblems and some type. (R.B. McKerrow came to exactly the same conclusion in *Printer's and Publisher's Devices in England and Scotland*.)

The emblem in question shows Opportunity or Fortune, and has the motto: Aut Nunci Aut Nunquam, which means:

"Now or **Never**"

### Romeo & Juliet Q2

The real story of how the play *Romeo & Juliet* came to the public eye is profoundly different from the fiction proposed by the movie *"Shakespeare in Love."* Shakespeare did not struggle to make up a plot. He took a pre-existing Italian story, added his own plot touches, and served the entire dish up in the flavor of his own sublime poetry.

This example of a "Shakespeare edited quarto" is particularly poignant because Shakespeare 's name is nowhere to be found. The First quarto of *R&J* was the notoriously "Bad" pirated version issued by John Danter in 1597.

Two years later Cuthbert Burby somehow got  hold of a much better text. Perhaps it was obtained by the printer he brought in for the job, Thomas Creede, a man pivotal to the thesis I am developing here.

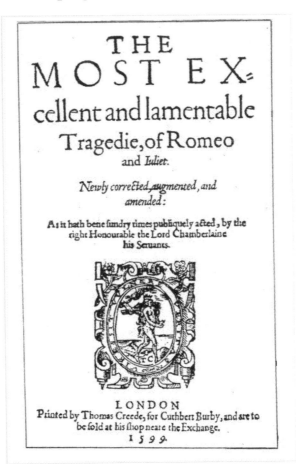

*Romeo and Juliet*, Q2,  title page.

The title page reads :

> The Most Excellent and lamentable Tragedie, of Romeo and Juliet
> Newly corrected, augmented, and amended:
> As it hath been sundry times publiquely acted,
> by the right Honourable the Lord Chamberlaine his Servants.
> Printed by Thomas Creede for Cuthbert Burby ... 1599.

So the first edition, 1597, says nothing about Shakespeare. The Q2, 1599, which claims to be "Newly corrected, augmented, and amended," and is in fact the authentic text of *R&J*, gives no-one credit, in spite of the fact that *Palladis Tamia*, published by Burby himself the year before, claimed *R&J* as a Shakespeare play. It boggles the mind. Meres couldn't have based his statement on the evidence of the existing books or manuscripts, and Burby, for some reason, did not take the advice of his own sister publication. This bears repeating: Cuthbert Burby, the publisher of *Palladis Tamia*, 1598, which credits Shakespeare with *Romeo & Juliet*, did not credit the play to Shakespeare when he himself obtained the true text of the play, in 1599 !

If Shakespeare's name had a commercial cachet associated with it, why was his name not used on this publication? If Shaksper of Stratford, the man allegedly eager for fortune and fame, took the time to provide Burby or Creede with his complete manuscript, why was he not paid or at least acknowledged in the publication. It makes no sense unless someone other than Shaksper or the theater owners was providing real texts to the printers.

Thomas Creede is crucial to this study because he is connected to accepted Shakespeare material, apocryphal Shakespeare material, and books linked to the Earl of Oxford. The most extraordinary example is *The Weakest Goeth to the Wall*, printed in 1600 by Creede. The title page blurb says.

*The Weakest Goeth to the Wall* As it hath bene sundry times played by the right honorable Earle of Oxenford, Lord great Chamberlaine of England his servants.

THE
VVEAKEST
goeth to the VVall.

*As it hath bene sundry times plaide by the right ho-nourable Earle of* Oxenford, *Lord great Chamberlaine of* England *his seruants.*

L·O·N·D·O·N
Printed by Thomas Creede, for Richard Oliue, dwelling in Long Lane.
1 6 0 0.

*The Weakest Goeth to the Wall*, title page.

The play is Anonymous. This is a key item of evidence because it clearly states  that this is a play from Oxford's company's repertoire. Although Oxford's name appears as a dedicatee in the very earliest of Creede's printed quartos (*Card of Fancy*), this is the first, and I believe, the only instance in which Oxford's name ever appears anywhere overtly on the title page of a printed play.

Thomas Creede used a unique block-print emblem or device for many, but not all of his books:
VIRESSIT  VVLNERE  VERITAS
Which means: **Truth is renewed through Wounding**. The device and Creede are discussed at length in Chapters 10 and 15.

Another interesting peculiarity about this Q2 edition of *R&J*, edited by the unnamed author, is that it has the line "enter Will Kempe" instead of "enter Peter" at Act 4, scene 5, line 102. A curious slip, naming the actor, rather than the character.

## Richard III Q3

The earlier publication history of *Richard the Third* is instructive:

The first quarto of *Richard III* came out Anonymously in 1597. The printer was Valentine Simmes and the publisher was Andrew Wise.

The Q2, 1598, also produced by Simmes and Wise is essentially the same as the first, with one key change. On the title page is added the credit: "By William Shake-speare."

In the case of *Richard the Third*, Q3, 1602, we have the statement that the text was "Newly augmented", but there are no particular additions or augmentations. The text does vary minutely from the two earlier editions, and the *Reader's Encyclopedia of Shakespeare* does make the claim that the *Folio* version of *Richard the Third* was influenced by the Q3 and the Q6 of 1622.

*Richard the Third* Q3, which claims to be augmented by the author in 1602, is in fact a definitive edition. The printer was Thomas Creede and the publisher was Andrew Wise, who effectively owned the rights to the play. But it is fascinating that in 2 out these 5 instances where a Shakespeare publisher switched printers and coincidentally obtained a true text of the play, the printer involved was Mr. Creede. We have the insinuation of a direct connection to the author of the Shakespeare plays.

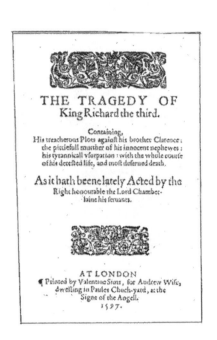

Title pages from *Richard III* Q 1 (left) and Q3 (right).

## Hamlet Q2

Hamlet first appeared in Quarto in 1603.

This Q1 is almost universally considered a "Bad" quarto because it does not contain the full text as presented in the Q2 of 1604. Also, much of the famous dialogue is significantly different from what we are used to in the standard text. One theory, not widely accepted, is that the 1603 *Hamlet* is based on a lost "ur-Hamlet", and that its anachronistic and outdated appearance in print prompted the author, a year later, to "release" the complete and updated play to the publisher, Nicholas Ling. The actual printer of *Hamlet Q1* is not named, but the publishers are listed as Nicholas Ling and John Trundell, both booksellers. I tend to agree with Eric Sams that the Q1 *Hamlet* is not really so "bad", so much as OLD. There was clearly an older, shorter play, current in the late 1580's, but played at the universities, not on the London stage. The Q1 title page says it was played at Oxford and Cambridge, so the standard story is that it had been played at the schools circa 1601-1602. It may have, but other than the title page statement, there isn't any corroborating evidence. It is more likely that the statement on Q1 represents a reminder of the plays' antiquity. The Stationers Registry entry for *Hamlet* in 1602 says 'lately played' ... which is an ambiguous statement. Is it not possible that a popular revival of the old *Hamlet* around 1602, coupled with the death of Queen Elizabeth the next year, gave Oxford the impetus, the motive means and opportunity to do the lengthy, complex rewrite? The expanded book was not published till King James was in charge. And it was possibly printed with Royal approval (because of the Arms of England on the inside page in Q2 1604). I've thought that Fortinbras may represent King James, who comes in from another country to provide a new royal line, ending the succession squabble. The character was possibly made into a semi-hero to flatter James.

In 1603, the bad or pirate version of *Hamlet* Q1 came out, (printed in part by Roberts), and published by Ling and Trundell. In 1604, the Q2, full-length, full-strength *Hamlet* came out, published by Ling and printed by James Roberts.

Many argue that *Hamlet* Q1 is a pirated text, a misheard and misremembered aberration of the full, real *Hamlet*, then current. This is the Pirate theory. In *Hamlet* Q1 vs. Q2, there is too much additional material in Q2 for Q1 to be simply a mis-remembering. Q1 is a faulty text perhaps, but not of the full and final *Hamlet*. But that's all on the level of literary interpretation. There are also facts in the case that weigh against the Pirate theory:

*Hamlet* was officially entered in the Stationers' Register by printer and agent James Roberts on July 26, 1602. The wording of the entry indicates that the item Roberts brought in and deposited was a book or bound manuscript, already pre-existing : ... " James Robertes. Entered for his Copie under the hands of master Pasefield and master Waterson, warden, a booke called *the Revenge of Hamlet Prince Denmark* as it was lately acted by the Lord Chamberleyne his servants"

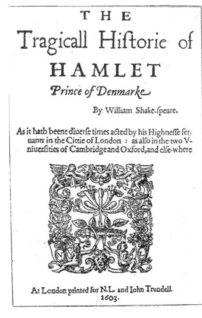

As brevity is the soul of wit, I shall be brief: the so called "pirates" were also the official printers and publishers. If the publisher Ling had committed a crime, legal or artistic, why did the author reward him with the new complete manuscript? If Q1 was a remembered text rushed into print to make a fast buck, why did James Roberts copyright a pre-existing text and then sit on it for a year?

If Roberts and Ling possessed the full text all along, why did Ling print the limited Q1? If Roberts and Ling had only the Q1 text in 1602 and 1603 then they probably published what they had. The author, in 1604, sparked by the play's reception, the Queens death, and his own mortality looming, either rewrote the play or released the full text for the first time to Roberts and Ling, now that the political climate had changed.

Anyway, that's my opinion, but it is based on the historical facts in the case, not on whether the Q1 "to be or not to be" speech seems  mangled to our ears, spoiled by the version we are accustomed to. The two versions may be up to  35 years apart in composition.

Amazingly, *Hamlet* has no verifiable stage history, at the Universities, or on the public stage until 1637.  There is a vague reference to a private performance on a boat in 1607, and to a possible Court performance in 1619. The performances mentioned on the title page of the first quarto of *Hamlet*, 1603, may or may not relate to performances in the 1590's ... it's unverifiable.

Perhaps the lost "Ur-Hamlet" was a play written by Oxford when he was still in College. Performances of the play in various forms certainly occurred in the 1580's or 90's.

By 1603 it was a very antique play .
In 1604 it became so modern it still seems modern.

If you really read the *Hamlet* first quarto text with an open mind, you may see that there is nothing wrong with the play. It is a completely coherent, engrossing Shakespeare play, it is just utterly different than the *Hamlet* we are accustomed to. It is a shorter, "lighter", more action driven script, and has less of the psychological and philosophical meanderings. Many of the key Shakespearean catch phrases are intact. The songs are intact. The ghost scene is intact, but not the line "truepenny".

My interpretation remains that the Q1 title page tells the truth (sort of) when it says the play was seen on the stages of Cambridge and Oxford.  It feels like a script for a college cast. It could easily be an early version of *Hamlet*, (late 1580's) that survived in MS unchanged until 1603. I am still persuaded that the earliest roots of *Hamlet* go back to Vere's own childhood, when he was called back from studies to attend his father's funeral, then endure his mother's remarriage. The lead character Hamlet is seen as a 14 or 15 year old at the beginning of the play. Many standard commentators have noticed that Hamlet seems to age by 10 or 20 years over the course of the full Q2 play, which actually only reflects a few weeks of real time action.

The title page blurb was rewritten for this second edition of *Hamlet*.

It claims:

> Newly imprinted and enlarged to almost as much againe as it was, according to the true and perfect Copie

## James Roberts and Oxford

James Roberts (1564-1606), a prolific printer, held the unique royal monopoly on the printing of Astrological almanacs and prognostications, His patent was granted on May 12, 1588, and lasted throughout the reign of Elizabeth. In May of 1594, James Roberts took over the business of John Charlewood, a man known to the Earl of Oxford from as early as 1580, when Charlewood printed the lavish and well financed *Zelauto*, which is dedicated to Oxford and bears the marks of his personal interest. Charlewood printed *Pandora*, 1584, by Oxfords' servant John Southern. *Pandora* is dedicated to Oxford and his wife, and contains verses written by Anne, the Countess Oxford. Charlewood was a key figure in the Marprelate controversy, and is mentioned by Martin in two of his tracts, *Oh Read over* and *the Epistle*. Martin claims that John Charlewood was "the Earl of Arundel's man". In 1595 James Roberts married the widow Alice Charlewood, and cemented his hold on Charlewood's former customer base and his patent rights. Roberts gained the lucrative patent on the printing of all theatrical Playbills.

The man who registered *Hamlet* and printed the *Hamlet* Q2 1604 masterpiece, also printed these Shakespeare books:

| | | | |
|---|---|---|---|
| *Hamlet* | Q3 | 1605 | (Good) |
| *Merchant of Venice* | Q1 | 1600 | (Good) |
| *Titus Andronicu* | Q2 | 1600 | (Good) |

One of my discoveries was that Roberts was involved with no less than five books that feature Edward de Vere in some way :

*Gwydonius, Carde of Fancie* Q2, by Robert Greene, 1587, printed by James Roberts for William Ponsonby. This has a classic dedication to the Earl of Oxford. Here Roberts is working for Ponsonby, just as Creede would be doing after him.

*Paradyse of Dainty Devises* Q7, by R. Edwardes, EO, etc., 1600, printed by James Roberts for E. White. In 1585 the bookseller Edward White purchased the rights to *Paradyse* from the original owner Henry Disle. White brought out reprints every few years, changing printers as needed. Thus in 1600, while Roberts was printing pages of "Shakespeare" (*Merchant* and *Titus*) he was also printing Oxford's poems in the revival edition of *Paradyse*.

*Euphues and his England* Q8, 1597 and Q9, 1601, printed by James Roberts for Gabriel Cawood. These were revival printings of a perennial best-seller that also has a long fawning introduction to Edward de Vere.

*England's Helicon*, 1600, credited to J. Bodenham, printed by James Roberts for John Flasket, contains the Ignoto poems and one poem directly credited to Oxford: "What shepherd can express..."

In 1602 James Roberts registered *Hamlet* and *Troilus and Cressida*, but both were delayed significantly. If Roberts didn't know Shakespeare, but received the texts in a straightforward deal with a theatrical person, there would be no reason for him to delay publication. The facts in the case suggest that Roberts knew the author personally, and was requested to hold the press on these books until further notice.

Though Roberts copyrighted *Hamlet* in 1602, he dis-avowed or refused participation in N. Ling's bad Q1, 1603. When the good text turned up, Roberts printed the Q2 , 1604, and proudly put his name (well, his initials) on it.

Everyone agrees that Hamlet Q2 has a text that is completely from the pen of Shakespeare (whoever he really was). This re-write, dated 1603-1604, is the last time that the author interacted directly with the printers in the name of Shakespeare. James Roberts was a man known and trusted by the Earl of Oxford.

## The Five Re-Written Texts

In the five instances we have looked at, either the author Shakespeare contributed true texts to the printers, or the theaters did, in his name. If one takes the cynical approach that this was only a marketing gimmick, one can not explain why *Romeo & Juliet Q2* fails to mention Shakespeare.

There were 13 Quarto publications from 1617-1623, any one of which might have alluded to the recent death of the author, or capitalized on it, if Shaksper's death in 1616 was really noticed by anyone in the literary or publishing worlds. The orthodox scholars are right about one thing: Shaksper-of-Stratford had nothing to do with the printing of the Shakespeare quartos.

Under the standard story of Shakespeare of Stratford, it is hard to explain why the author would disappear from the publishing world at the peak of his renown, and live in invisible retirement for 12 more years, writing classic plays that were neither performed or printed. In the Oxfordian scenario, Edward de Vere's death in 1604 is the reason that the Author known as Shakespeare was out of the loop after 1604.

The majority of Shakespeare first quartos and corrected quartos occurred during the final decade of Oxford's life. After 1604 the pipeline to Shakespeare was shut off. All of the "post 1604" plays can be demonstrated to actually date from the 1580's and 1590's.

Reviewing the printers and sellers who are named on both Oxford Books and "Shakespeare Books" (for space, only one or two examples is given in each category):

| Stationer | Oxford Book | Shakespeare Book |
|---|---|---|
| Cuthbert Burby | Eng. Secr. , Axiochus | LLL Q1, R&J Q2 |
| Thomas Creede | Weakest Goeth, "Card" | R&J Q2, RIII Q3 |
| John Danter | Tears of Fancy, Axiochus | R&J Q1, Titus Q1 |
| Richard Field | Ecclesiastes, Courtier | V&A, Lucrece |
| John Harrison | Defense of Military 1579 | V&A, Lucrece |
| James Roberts | "Card", "Paradyse" | Hamlet, Merchant |
| Peter Short | New & Old Physic | H4thP1, H6thP3 |
| Simon Stafford | Anagrammata | H4thP1 Q2, Pericles Q2 |
| Edward White | "Paradyse" Q4-Q8 | Titus Q1 - Q3 |

## Exceptions and Anomalies

If we expand our data pool to include plays in the Shakespeare Apocrypha, we can add one more instance of claimed Shakespearean revisions. The play *Locrine* from 1595 claims:

> Newly set foorth, overseene and corrected
> By W.S.
> Printed by Thomas Creede

If Locrine is ever ranked as part of Shakespeare's output, second tier, the 1595 publication would be the first of SIX examples of claimed authorial revisions 1595 - 1604.

To be completely fair, a few examples in the later Shakespeare reprints might qualify as exceptions.

The Fifth edition of *The Rape of Lucrece* Q5, printed in 1616, says "Newly revised". Nobody believes that those revisions were authorial.

"The Whole contention" of 1619 (part of the notorious Jaggard 'false folio'), which repackaged several old Shakespeare plays, claimed: "Newly corrected and enlarged"

The third Quarto of *the Passionate Pilgrim* 1612, by Jaggard says "Newly corrected and augmented". But no one thinks Shakespeare had anything to do with *the Passionate Pilgrim* anyway.

These three exceptions are irrelevant because Shaksper of Stratford was dead himself, before *Lucrece* Q5, and the *Whole Contention* 1619. And *Passionate Pilgrim* is not a part of the accepted Canon.

# Chapter Eight
## The Early Shakespeare Quartos: Who's Who

"Officially" 19 authentic Shakespeare plays were issued in Quarto prior to the *Folio* of 1623. The number is higher if one accepts *Taming of a Shrew*, 1594 or other apocryphal quartos. Of those 19 publications, 15 emerged from 1594 to 1603. Considering just these publications, there are at least 7 different printers and 10 booksellers named, and thus presumed to be "involved".

The following are the Printers of Shakespeare Play First Editions from 1594 to 1603:

**Thomas Creede** printed *Henry the Sixth Part 2*, Q1, 1594, and the first "Good" Quarto, (the Q2), of *Romeo & Juliet* in 1599. He printed *Henry the Fifth*, Q1, in 1600 . These plays all appeared Anonymously. Creede also printed the "bad" Q1 of *Merry Wives of Windsor*, 1602, which was the first instance where Creede used the credit: "William Shakespeare". Creede printed the Q2, Q3, Q4, and Q5 of *Richard III* . Thomas Creede also printed many other books relevant to the Oxford/Shake-speare hypothesis, and he is clearly linked to Edward de Vere. These connections are discussed at length elsewhere in this study.

**John Danter** printed *Titus Andronicus*, Q1, 1594 and *Romeo & Juliet*, Q1, 1597. Both quartos were Anonymous. John Danter once got in big trouble for printing Catholic devotionals. He later became a partner with Henry Chettle, who was another key player in the 1590's Literary scene. Danter, who was the son of an Oxfordshire weaver, may have interested Oxford. Danter is the printer of two Oxford related books. *The Tears of Fancy*, 1593, contains a poem by Oxford: "Who taught me first to sigh".

Danter also printed *Axiochus*, 1592 which contains the text of a speech Oxford wrote for a Tournament oration. Both these books were one-shots with no later editions. Danter printed Nashe's *Terrors of the Night*, 1594, and *Have with you to Saffron*

*Walden*, 1596, which states that Nashe was living in the same household as Mr. and Mrs. Danter. Gabriel Harvey attacked both Danter and Nashe in print, calling the satirist "Danter's Gentleman" and "Danter's Maulkin". Most significantly, Danter was the printer of Nashe's *Strange Newes*, 1592, which has an elaborate dedication to a man referred to as Apis Lapis. This Apis Lapis can be shown to be the Earl of Oxford. John Danter printed the anonymous *Fair Em*, 1591, which is considered a Shakespearean Apocrypha. Danter printed Chettle's *Kind Heart's Dreame*, 1593, which contains a response to attacks made in *Groatsworth of Wit*. Standard scholars see Chettle's statements as a defense of Shakespeare, but he does not mention the dramatist by name. Danter, who died around 1598, was featured as a character in the 1606 University play *The Return from Parnassus*. Danter says to the character Ingenioso:

> It's true; but good faith, Master Ingenioso, I lost by your last book: and you know there is many one that pays me largely for the printing of their inventions; but for all this, you shall have forty shillings, and an odd pottle of wine.

**James Roberts'** career spanned four decades. He became a freeman of the Guild in 1564. He printed ballads, almanacks, and by marriage to the widow of John Charlewood, he obtained the exclusive rights to print playbills. Roberts was the printer of *Merchant of Venice*, Q1, 1600. He printed the *Titus* Q2 in 1600. Roberts was the man who entered *Hamlet* in the Stationers' Register in 1602, and printed the "good" or enlarged *Hamlet* , Q2 of 1604. Roberts sold his business to William Jaggard, who printed many "Shakespeare" Quartos, including some falsely backdated, in 1619. The Jaggard family participated in the printing of the *First Folio* in 1623. Roberts is strongly linked to the Earl of Oxford, as explained in Chapter 7.

**Peter Short** became a freeman of the Stationers in 1589. He was the printer of *Henry the Sixth Part 3*, Q1, 1595, and *Henry the Fourth Part 1*, Q1, 1598 . Both of these plays appeared anonymously. Peter Short was also the printer of *Palladis*

*Tamia*, 1598, by Meres. This important book lists Oxford as the greatest comedic dramatist, and also launches the "Shakespeare" pen-name (as an attributed playwright). Short also printed *The Taming of a Shrew*, Q1, 1594, the source play which is still unaccepted by orthodoxy as Shakespeare's. In the Oxford scenario, this anonymous play was de Vere's early version. Short's link to Oxford is based on two books printed in 1599: *The English Secretary*, Q4, revised and updated by Angel Daye with a new dedication to de Vere, *and The Practice of New and Old Physic*, by George Baker, 1599, an alchemy and medicine book written by Oxford's doctor, and now updated with a new dedication to Edward de Vere. *New and Old Physic* was an update on Bakers' original book: *The new Jewel of Health*, 1576 which had a dedication to de Vere's wife, Anne Cecil de Vere, the Countess Oxford. The printer in 1576 had been Henrie Denham. Peter Short took over Denham's business, and his customers.

**Valentine Simmes** apprenticed with Henry Bynneman during the era in which Bynneman produced several books for Oxford which were presented to his wife Anne. *Golden Epistles*, by Geoffrey Fenton, 1582, was the third and final edition of a well printed book dedicated to Countess Oxford. *St. John Chrysotom ... upon the Epistle to the Ephesians*, dated Dec. 24, 1581 on the title page was another religious work dedicated to Anne Oxford. Simmes became a freeman of the Company in 1585. He did not encounter "Shakespeare" texts until 12 years later. Simmes printed *Richard the Second*, Q1, anonymous, 1597. A year later he produced the Q2 of *Richard the Second*, with the empty credit now filled with "by William Shake-speare". Simmes printed *Richard the Third*, Q1, anonymous, in 1597. Simmes printed *Henry the Fourth Part 2*, Q1 and *Much Ado about Nothing*, Q1, in 1600. Simmes was another "troublemaker" (to the authorities). He had been arrested in the strange "Martin Marprelate" pamphlet war and scandal of the late 1580's. He was named in 1599 as one of 14 printers forbidden, by Star Chamber decree, from printing any more Satires or Epigrams.

**William White** was a printer who was active in the business from 1597 to 1615. W. White was the printer of two Shakespeare first editions, *Love's Labors Lost*, in 1598, and *Pericles* in 1609. White usually printed music and ballads. He brought out three quarto reprints of Shakespeare plays.

* No printer is named on *Midsummer Night's Dream*, Q1, 1600. Which simply says "Printed <u>for</u> Thomas Fisher, bookseller". The modern *Short Title Catalogue* indicates that the unnamed printer might by R. Bradocke.

* Similarly, no printer is named on the Q1 "bad" *Hamlet*, 1603. Nicholas Ling was the named seller/publisher. One possible printer was James Roberts, who registered *Hamlet* and printed the Q2. And some scholarship indicates that Roberts printed at least a portion of the 1603 edition. *The Short Title Catalogue* now credits the main printer of Hamlet Q1 as Valentine Simmes.

The following are the Shakespeare Q1 Booksellers in the era 1594 to 1603:

**William Aspley** became a freeman of the Stationers' Company in 1597 and was active as a bookseller from 1598 to 1640. He is named as the seller on: *Henry the Fourth, Part 2,* Q1, 1600, and *Much Ado about Nothing* Q1, 1600. Aspley is perhaps most significant as one of the named booksellers of SHAKE-SPEARES SONNETS of 1609. George Eld and Thomas Thorpe were the printers, but Aspley actually sold the *Sonnets* and made whatever significant money there was to be had on the enterprise. Aspley was successful later with such plays as *Eastward Ho*, by Jonson, Chapman, and Marston.

**Cuthbert Burby** was a bookseller who flourished from 1592 to 1607. Burby had apprenticed with William Wright, the publisher of an Oxford-dedicated book, *Palmerin d'Oliva part 1*, 1588, Q1. Burby became a Freeman of the Stationers' in 1592. Burby was the seller of *Loves Labors Lost* Q1, 1598, and the full text 2$^{nd}$ Quarto of *Romeo & Juliet*, in 1598, printed by

Creede. Burby published the controversial *Taming of A Shrew*, 1594.

**John Busby** was a bookseller who was active from 1590 to 1619. He has a reputation as a second-rate publisher, and his principal link to the Shakespeare books is that he is named as one of two sellers of the "bad" first quarto of *Henry the Fifth* in 1600. But Busby's name also appears in the Stationers' Register as having entered *The Merry Wives of Windsor* and assigning the copyright to Arthur Johnson on Jan. 18, 1602. Busby was also one of the original copyright holders of *King Lear*, which he registered on Nov. 26, 1607 with Nathaniel Butter. The book came out the following year without Busby's name.

**Thomas Fisher** is named as the seller or publisher of *Midsummer Nights Dreame*, Q1, 1600. Like Simon Stafford, Fisher was originally a draper, but won admittance as a freeman of the Stationers' Company in 1600, just in time to publish the Shakespeare play.

**Thomas Heyes** (or Hayes) had a very short but significant career as a publisher and bookseller. His first entry in the Stationers' Register was in 1600 for the poetry collection *England's Parnassus*. This huge anthology contains 3 poems credited to the Earl of Oxford: "What plague is greater than the grief of mind", "Doth Sorrow fret thy Soul", and "Love is a discord and a strange divorce". *England's Parnassus* also contains known Shakespeare poetry, but ambiguously credited, and thus the book is rarely cited as being a part of the "legitimate Shakespeare books", if there are such things. Heyes' link to the Shakespeare plays is through one work, *The Merchant of Venice*.

*Merchant* was officially entered to James Roberts on July 22, 1598. The copyright was assigned to Thomas Heyes on Oct 28, 1600. The quarto appeared that month. Roberts is the named printer; he clearly obtained the good text (from somewhere), sold the rights to Heyes, and then printed the book, making money from both the contract work, and the sale of copyright. Heyes died sometime before February, 1604, when his wife sold some copyrights to Humphrey

Lownes. The rights to *Merchant of Venice* eventually went to Heyes' son Lawrence. When William Jaggard re-published *Merchant of Venice* in 1619, he falsely back dated the quarto to read 1600, in an attempt to circumvent the ownership of Lawrence Heyes. Heyes complained after Jaggard's fraud and re-registered the book himself. Presumably Jaggard obtained the rights to *Merchant* in 1623 when the *Folio* was assembled, but not necessarily, because in 1637, Lawrence Heyes printed the play himself without fine.

**Arthur Johnson** was a bookseller whose name appears on publications from 1602 to 1630. His singular Shakespeare project was the flawed quarto of *The Merry Wives of Windsor*, 1602, printed by Thomas Creede. The two men republished *Merry Wives* in 1619. Interestingly, in 1617, it was Arthur Johnson who published the first combined version of *Euphues Anatomy of Wit* and *Euphues and His England* by John Lyly, the combined book containing a long dedication to Edward de Vere.

**Nicholas Ling** was a bookseller active from 1580 to 1607. He apprenticed with Henry Bynneman in the 1570's. It is interesting to note that during his apprenticeship with Bynneman, Ling must have worked on the *Gratulationis Valdinensis*, 1578, by Gabriel Harvey, which contains the long homage to Edward de Vere and refers to him as a man so intense his "will shakes spears". Oxford-dedicated books printed by Bynneman during Ling's apprenticeship also include: *Peisistratus and Catanea*, 1570, by Edmund Elviden, and *The Courtier in Latin* Q2, 1577.

Nicholas Ling is also credited as the editor of the *Politeuphuia, Wits Commonwealth*, 1597, which is the companion volume to *Palladis Tamia, Wit's Treasury*, 1598. It is un-provable, but possible that Ling was one of the un-credited editors of *Palladis Tamia*, the book that praises Oxford as the best comic dramatist, and then introduces this unknown new man, "Shakespeare" as the new bright light. Ling published the "bad quarto" of *Hamlet*, 1603, and the full text quartos of 1604 and 1605.

**Thomas Millington** was a bookseller and publisher who was marginally active from 1593 to 1603. His name appears on only about 15 publications in total. He is named as the seller of 4 Shakespeare first editions: *Henry the Sixth, Part 2*, Q1, 1594, *Henry the Sixth, Part 3*, Q1, 1594, *Titus Andronicus*, Q1, 1594, and *Henry the Fifth*, Q1, 1600. Millington published *England's Mourning Garment* in 1603, a long Elegy to Queen Elizabeth, credited to Henry Chettle. The work is so entirely in the language and mindset of Oxford, however, that it may turn out to be the real Shakespeare's tribute to his dead Queen.

**Edward White** was a bookseller who was actively in the business from 1577 to 1612. White was mostly a printer of ballads, but he did print literature and he has a link to the Earl of Oxford. *The Paradyse of Dainty Devises* was a poetry collection that features Edward de Vere and was first published by Henry Disle in 1576. The book proved popular and Disle contracted three more printings. The copyright was assigned from Disle to T. Rider in 1582, and from Rider to Edward White on April 11, 1584. White published sell-out editions in 1585, 1590, 1596, and 1600. The only Shakespeare book Edward White published was *Titus Andronicus*, Q1, 1594 with Millington as co-publisher and Danter as printer; the Q2 of 1600, White with James Roberts, and the *Titus* Q3 of 1611.

**Andrew Wise** was an active publisher and bookseller from 1589 to 1603. He had access to several Shakespeare plays that began anonymously. He published *Richard the Second* Q1, 1597, and *Richard the Third* Q1, 1597. Both were anonymous that year, but when Wise republished them both in 1598, he added a line crediting "William Shake-speare." Wise published *Henry the Fourth, Part 1* Q1, 1598, and does not name an author. Wise and Simmes published *Henry the Fourth, Part 2*, Q1, and *Much Ado about Nothing*, Q1, in 1600.

In Chapter 7, I discussed the five quartos in which Shakespeare, whoever he was, is claimed as editor or reviser. Two of those books are Wise publications: *Henry the 4^{th} Part*

*1*, Q2, 1599 (with Simon Stafford)  and *Richard III*, Q3, 1602 printed by Thomas Creede.

## Censorship and Secrecy

The printer's trade was tightly controlled and monitored through Her Majesty's government. Nothing was to be printed without approval, and all publications were to be entered first at the Stationers' Register. Nevertheless, many broadsheets, pamphlets and quartos did see print without passing the Stationers' censor. In some cases the printers or authors were prosecuted and jailed for unauthorized or treasonable publications. Remember that this era, the late 1500's, was the height of religious and economic rivalry between the Catholic states and the Protestant ones, especially England. Any un-sanctioned poem, play, or philosophical tract could theoretically harbor criticism of Elizabeth, or Papal propaganda, or a hundred other threats.

For authors and printers, producing works in this climate of paranoia was a dangerous business. It is not surprising therefore that some writers used pseudonyms for their works.  In some cases, poetry and dramas were published with no author cited at all.

Because of the atmosphere of censorship and danger in which the printers' technologies developed, the craft and trades of papermaking, typemaking, typesetting, engraving, and printing became a closed and semi-secret society of related guilds. The trades and trade-secrets typically remained within families over long stretches of time. Because of censorship of their work, printers had developed a variety of methods by which they could covertly express things. Watermarks in paper are the oldest method. Emblems, symbolic Devices, repetitive block prints, and type-setting were used extensively to convey coded or symbolic information.

In the Elizabethan era, the majority of small books and pamphlets were printed in the form of "Quartos", so called because each page was one quarter of the size of a standard piece of printers paper. A typical quarto was 9" tall, 7" wide. Following standard bibliographic practice, first quartos are now referred to as "Q1"; and a second printing is "Q2" etc.

Our knowledge of the history of the early Shakespeare Quartos is limited by the evidence that remains. So if it is stated that the 1594 *Titus Andronicus* is the first "Shakespearean" play in print, it must be understood that it is likely that earlier editions of some of the dramas existed, but are now either long lost, deeply hidden away, or as yet unrecognized. In this study I will deal with some of the documents that are available, specifically the early quartos, mostly anonymous, of the stage plays that later became known as Shakespeare's. The unknown dates of original composition will not be considered.

In this portion of my study I will focus on clues in the authorship puzzle which have been, up to now, largely ignored. These clues are found on the title pages of the earliest editions of the works generally referred to as Shakespeare's plays and poems. There are clues in the curious designs, wordings, graphic devices, and Latin inscriptions that are a steady feature of these books. Clues about the author's identity and social connections are also to be found from looking closely at the men who were commissioned to print and sell the books (and those who seem to have pirated some works).

The Shakespearean Quartos are delightful examples of English Renaissance printing and engraving techniques. It was the incredible variety and detailing of these quartos, especially the title pages, that led me to investigate them as thoroughly as possible. The unique research presented here looks at the striking curiosities found on the title pages of these famous works and discovers there perhaps the various (verius) signatures of the True author.

# Chapter Nine

## Edward de Vere's Name and Its Associations

In the Quarto material we are about to examine, many of the clues relate to the personal name of the 17th Earl of Oxford, Edward de Vere, and puns, in English and Latin, on the name Vere.

Below is pictured the simplest Coat of Arms of the de Vere family. The Motto:   VERO  NIHIL  VERIUS means
                "Nothing is Truer than Truth", or
                "Truly, nothing is Truer".

**De Vere family Coat of Arms.**

Note the two wild Boars on the emblem. In medieval Latin, and in Heraldry the word for Boar was "Verres".

The Latin word for wild is "Fer". So let us consider :

## Key Words and Puns that are Relevant to this Inquiry:

| In Latin | Meaning | Related English words |
|---|---|---|
| Venus | The Goddess Venus | Venus, venereal |
| veprecula | a small briar bush | a thorn bush, a bramble bush |
| ver | spring, springtime | vernal equinox, Primavera |
| vere | truly, really, rightly | verily |
| vereor | to have respect or awe for | revere |
| veritas | the Truth | veritable, verity |
| vero | in fact, truly, certainly | Veronica (+icon=true image) |
| Verona | a true place, a green place | Two gentlemen of Verona |
| verres | a boar | |
| verro | to drag, sweep, catch, collect | |
| verto | to turn, revolve, change | vertigo, advertising, convert |
| vir | a man, a strong man | virile |
| vireo | to be green | |
| viresco | to become green, to emerge | |
| viridis | the color green | viridian |
| virtus | excellence, manliness | virtue |
| fer | wild | feral (note "Master Fer" in *Henry the Fifth*, Act IV, scene 4) |
| ferox | brave | ferocious |

The following English words, puns on different pronunciations of "Vere", its meanings, or built on those puns, will become relevant as we proceed :

Very Fair Ever True Green

Edward de Vere studied Latin as a boy with his uncle Arthur Golding. The first English verse version of *Ovid's Metamorphoses*, with a translation credited to Golding, is the classic that is said to have been Shakespeare's principle inspiration. Ironically, the likely truth is that young de Vere was himself the chief author and wit behind the Golding version, and thus "inspired" his own later works. Oxford was immersed in the world of Ancient Latin, and drenched in Greco-Roman Mythology. As a boy, thumbing through a Latin dictionary, he couldn't help but notice that Venus was followed closely by Ver. The only word of note lurking between Venus and Ver is Vepres, a thorn bush. An

116

interesting image is here: The earthy god-man of spring (Ver) is eternally separated from his Goddess of love (Venus), by a bramble bush (Vepres).

> The thorny brambles and embracing bushes
> As fearful of him, part : through whom he rushes.
> *Venus & Adonis* 629-630

> The lanthorn (lantern) is the moon : I, the man in the moon ; this thorn bush, my thorn bush
>> *Midsummer Nights Dream* : 5 / 1 / 263

# Chapter Ten

# The Anonymous "Shakes-speare" Quartos in Detail

| Quarto | Year | G/B | Printer | Publisher |
|---|---|---|---|---|
| *Titus Andronicus* Q1 | 1594 | Good | Danter | White & Millington |
| *Henry the Sixth, P. 2* Q1 <br>The First Part of the Contention | 1594 | Bad | Creede | Millington |
| *Taming of A Shrew* Q1 | 1594 | Apoc. | Short | Burby |
| *Henry the Sixth, P. 3* Q1 <br>The True Tragedy of Richard ... | 1595 | Bad | Short | Millington |
| *Richard the Second* Q1 | 1597 | Good | Simmes | Wise |
| *Richard the Third* Q1 | 1597 | Good | " & Short | Wise |
| *Romeo and Juliet* Q1 | 1597 | Bad | Danter | Danter |
| *Henry the Fourth, P. 1* Q1 | 1598 | Good | Short | Wise |
| *Romeo and Juliet* Q2 | 1599 | Good | Creede | Burby |
| *Henry the Sixth, P. 3* Q2 <br>The True Tragedy of Richard ... | 1600 | Bad | White | Millington |
| *Titus Andronicus* Q2 | 1600 | Good | Roberts | Edward White |
| *Henry the Fifth* Q1 | 1600 | Bad | Creede | Millington & Busby |
| *Henry the Sixth, P. 2* Q2 <br>The First Part of the Contention | 1600 | Bad | Simmes | Millington |
| *Henry the Fifth* Q2 | 1602 | Bad | Creede | Pavier |
| *Romeo and Juliet* Q3 | 1609 | Good | Windet | Smethwicke |
| *Titus Andronicus* Q3 | 1611 | Good | Allde | Edward White |
| *Romeo and Juliet* Q4 | 1622 | Good | Stansby | Smethwicke |

## Titus Andronicus

Titus Andronicus first appeared in Quarto in 1594. No author is named on the title page. *Titus* remained anonymous through three editions over 17 years, in spite of Meres' claim that *Titus* was a "William Shakespeare" play in 1598.

This *Titus* quarto mentions the Earls of Derby, Pembroke, and Sussex, three men closely tied to the 17th Earl of Oxford, in both the House of Lords, and as fellow patrons of dramatic companies. The printer was John Danter, and the publishers were E. White and T. Millington.

*Titus Andronicus* Q1, title page.

The woodcut emblem used on this title page is rectangle of scrollwork with an oval inset. The Figure portrayed is a naked woman who is meant to be turning on a wheel. Revolving or turning is "verto". She has long hair in the front and is bald on the back of her head. The World, as symbolized by the Sea, a Ship, and Mountains, goes on around her. Her circular scarf also symbolizes turning, the seasons, the wheel of the year. What does this curious image mean? Fortunately there is a documented answer. The image on this printer's block is an adaptation of an emblem that appeared in the 1586 book by Geoffrey Whitney: *A Choice of Emblemes and Other Devises*. Whitney, who lived from 1548 to 1601, was a contemporary of de Vere. His book portrays symbolic emblems and has poems that accompany, to explain the images. This emblematic figure there is called "Occasion" or "Opportunity", and the idea is that when opportunity presents "herself" to you, grab her firmly by the hair (that is, take action). Because if you delay, and she passes you by, you won't have anything to grab, as she is bald on the back of her head. The general meaning of this Emblem then, is "seize the moment". But "carpe diem" or other similar Latin maxims do not appear on this emblem.

Instead, the Inscription around the oval reads:
  "AVT NVNCI AVT NVNQVAM "
This translates unequivocally as: " Now or Never ".

**"Occasion" emblem.** Use with motto on Titus Andronicus title page (left), prior use by Whitney (center) and Alciati (right).

"Now or Never" fits the meaning of the emblem and it allows for the word "Never" to be indicated. As we will see, "Never" is a code word used often in the Plays, and on the Title pages. "Never" contains several significant puns and ciphers :

* **Ne Ver** ...    "ne" in Latin usually refers to negation, but often, when used as an interjection, it means "Certainly" or "Truly" or "Verily". In English we say "Not true?"
So "Ne Ver" can be read as "Verily Ver" or "Truly True"

* **N. e Ver** ...  "N." is often short for "Nomine" or "Name"
  "N. e Ver" thus alludes to "Name : E Ver"

* **Nee Ver**    ... This I admit is more far fetched. "Nee" is a French word,  derived from Latin, which means a  woman's maiden name. Or , more generally, it can mean:  "previously known as". So "Nee Ver" becomes  "previously known as Ver".

The Motto *Aut Nunci Aut Nunquam* is not associated with Whitney's emblem, or the earlier Opportunity emblem by Alciati. Whoever cut the printer's block for John Danter added a new twist. Its first "Shakespeare-related" use, on *Titus Andronicus*, is perhaps apt, as the hero of that drama, Titus, does indeed have terribly bad luck, growing out of not seizing an opportunity.

The words "Fortune" and "occasion" are highly favored by Shakespeare, which you can see for yourself with a Concordance, or a computer text version of the Canon. While you are at it,  look up "fair" "true" "very" "truly" etc. which run to hundreds of entries.

Shakespeare was aware of the myth behind the emblem:

PISTOL:     Bardolph, a soldier, firm and sound of heart,
            And of buxom valour, hath by cruel fate,
            **And giddy Fortune's furious fickle wheel,**
            **That goddess blind,**
            **That stands upon the rolling restless stone–**
            *Henry the 5ᵗʰ* Act III, scene 6

EMILIA:              ...The Moor replies,
                     That he you hurt is of great fame in Cyprus,
                     And great affinity, and that in wholesome wisdom
                     He might not but refuse you; but he protests he loves you
                     And needs no other suitor but his likings
                     **To take the safest occasion by the front**
                     **To bring you in again**.
                     *Othello* Act III, Scene 1

## John Danter and *Metamorphoses*

*The 15 books of Ovid's Metamorphoses*, as translated by Golding (and, I believe young Oxford) has an interesting publication history. The work first appeared as the *The first four books of ... Metamorphoses*, 1565, which was printed by William Seres, the master Stationer, a man well known to Edward de Vere in his student days. Two years later the work was completed and the first full book appeared: *The 15 books of P. Ovidus Naso entitled Metamorphoses*, Q1, 1567. Seres printed the Q2 in 1575. In the 1580's, ownership of the book was transferred to Henrie Denham, a man known by the Earl and Countess Oxford for his incredible job of printing *The New Jewel of Health*, 1576 with its numerous woodcut illustrations. In January 1584, Denham yielded his copyright to *Metamorphoses* to the Stationers' Company. After that, five later editions came out over 28 years, each time by a different print shop. Perhaps ambitious printers with financial backing for the project appealed to the Stationers' for the right to print *Metamorphoses* as a one-shot. Or it is possible that someone with access to the highest levels of the Stationers' Company said: "It's time for another edition of Ovid. Here's ten pounds. Get the job done."

*Metamorphoses* Q3, 1584, was printed by Windet & Judson
*Metamorphoses* Q4, 1587, was printed by **Robert Walde-grave**
*Metamorphoses* Q5, 1593, was printed by **John Danter**
*Metamorphoses* Q6, 1603, was printed by William White
*Metamorphoses* Q7, 1612, was printed by Thomas Purfoot

Walde-grave was the first printer (1586) of *The English Secretary*, an important book about writing and reasoning by Oxford's Secretary, Angel Daye. The book is dedicated to Oxford and looks like he paid for it. Danter's edition features the Green Man Emblem.

So the edition of *Ovid's Metamorphoses* that was "in print and available" in the 1590's was Danter's version. The 1567 First edition title page has a blurb:

A worke very pleasaunt and delectable.

In 1575, the spelling by Seres is modified:
A Worke very pleasant and delectable.

On Danter's version of 1593:
A worke **verie** pleasant and delectable.

This Opportunity device, as a printer's emblem, is identified by McKerrow as #281. He cites its first known use as the Danter quarto "*Jurisprudentiae ...*" by H. Smith, 1592. This was one of many sermons and religious tracts by Henry Smith, also known as "the silver tongued Smith", a significant Protestant intellectual, and a contemporary, and distant relative of Oxford. But it is premature to conclude that Danter's emblem was cut for the Smith book, or actually used there first. We may be missing earlier uses.

The emblem does appear on several books that seem to be "of a piece" with the Shakespeare-Oxford nexus. Opportunity graces Nashe's *Terrors of the Night*, 1594, and the anonymous but fractured text of *Romeo and Juliet* Q1, 1597. After Danter died, or went into witness-protection in 1598, his emblems and type passed to Simon Stafford. Stafford used the Opportunity (Now or Never) emblem on the "corrected by Shake-speare" *Henry the 4ᵗʰ Part 1*, Q2 , of 1599.

## Henry the Sixth, Part 2

*Henry the Sixth, Part 2* first appeared in Quarto form in 1594. The full title as given is *The First part of the Contention betwixt the two famous Houses of Yorke and Lancaster, with the death of the good Duke Humphrey ... "*, but the text correlates with *Henry the Sixth, Part 2*.

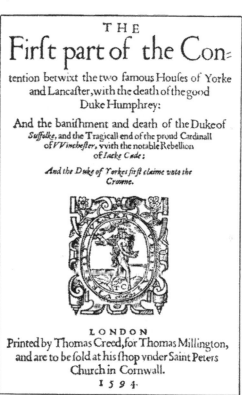

*Henry VI* Q1 title page.

The printer is Thomas Creede and the publisher is Millington again. This item is generally considered to be a "Bad Quarto", because the text is so extremely variant from the *Folio* version. But in a different paradigm of how the Shakespeare plays evolved, this play: *The First part of the Contention,* is a genuine printing of an archaic touring version of the play. Note that there is no Author credit.

The distinctive feature of the Title page is a rectangular Emblem containing within it an oval crest. The dominant image is a naked, crowned Goddess. A hand from a cloud above scourges her and goads her onward. She holds a book protectively in her hands. From the Latin motto we learn this Goddess is named " Truth " (Veritas)

The inscription reads : VIRESSIT  VVLNERE  VERITAS
Virescit is:  Sprouting, Greening, Emerging, or Springing
Vulnere is:  wounded, or from her wound
Veritas is: The Truth

**"Wounded Truth" emblem,** from *Henry VI* Q1 title page.

Acceptable Translations are:

"By wounding, Truth is renewed,"
"Truth grows again through wounding"
"Truth springs from Her wound "

The "Vir" in Virescit is "maleness" or "green". Virescit derives from "vireo" (to be green) , and "viresco" (becoming green, sprouting). And "Ver" is "Spring" or "True". Both words are a tip towards Edward de Vere, whose motto of course is Vero Nihil Verius. The double appearance of the "Ver" pun in "Viressit Vulnere Veritas" is not easy to ignore.

There is more: "Viressit", as it is presented, is possibly misspelled on the inscription. Correct Latin would give "Virescit ", which could have a hard "sk" sound as in "skit". Perhaps the misspelling is on purpose to create the pun "Vir ess it" ... i.e. "Vere is it" .

Viressit Vulnere Veritas in initials is " V.V.V. ". The "vu" in "vulnere" is given as " V V ". We will see "V. V." in many other forms on the Quartos.

Here are two examples of Edward de Vere's handwritten signature.

In each signature here you will notice a little zig-zag figure, VVV, directly above "Edward Oxenford". This looks very much like VVV or VNV.

If it is VNV it may stand for Vero Nihil Verius.
If it is VVV it may relate to Viressit Vulnere Veritas.

It may of course be just an innocent squiggle. A lot of Oxfordian ink has been spilled over whether the VVV is a depiction of a crown or coronet. An Earl's coronet, by Heraldic convention, should show 5 pearls or points on top. Oxford's unique glyph always shows 4 accentuated points. My contribution to the discussion is the conjecture that VVV may be the initials to a motto, in addition to whatever else they may represent. " V V " also finds a place as the "VV" in " VVilliam " which we will see was often used even when the printers possessed a proper "W".

VIRESSIT, in the spelling of the emblem,   gives an interesting anagram in plain English:

$$V \; i \; r \; e \; s \; s \; i \; t \; = \; it \; is \; Ver's$$

This "Truth" Emblem was the property of the printer, Thomas Creede. The initials "T.C." are there, by Truth's feet. Of course it's impossible to know whether the emblem is of Creede's own design, or was supplied to him by an author's agent for use on certain publications. There is, however, a small record of scholarship on Creede and this emblem, primarily from the pen of Ronald B. McKerrow, whose master work on emblems is *Printers and Publishers devices in England & Scotland 1485 - 1640* (London, 1913). This book has helped me to sort out fantasy from reality with regard to the history of the use of these devices. McKerrow identifies each emblem, traces it through the hands of various printers, and tries to indicate the first and last known uses. His data were limited by the quartos he had access to, circa 1913. Now many other early quartos have come to light, and fortunately, virtually all of the early English books have been microfilmed and roughly catalogued. Thus I have found significant emblem examples, apparently missed by McKerrow.

The "Wounded Truth" emblem is #299 in McKerrow's book. Explaining the significance of this emblem and the numerous important books it graced involves a large digression which is the subject of Part Four: Wounded Truth is Renewed.

The Truth emblem has an echo in *Minerva Britanna*, 1612. Several of Peacham's emblems and poems in *Minerva Britanna* seem to relate retroactively to the Earl of Oxford and to the images from the Shakespeare Quartos. The most obvious of the lot is shown on the next page.

The title is Veritas, TRUTH.

The figure seems to relate to the "Wounded Truth" of the Emblem called "Viressit Vulnere Veritas". But this Goddess is not being scourged or goaded from above. Now "Truth" is portrayed as above the earth, in Heaven. She holds a book, and pen, and one foot rests on the Globe. Which Veritas wrote for the Globe?

A tree stump is portrayed, with a new sprout of growth emerging. The same image again : Truth, though severely wounded or cut off, re-sprouts with vigor. The tree Stump was also the heraldic badge of Thomas of Woodstock, a hero of English history who was one of Edward de Vere's ancestors. The ornamental snakes surrounding the image spell " OXOXOXOX " .

In the little triangular device (at the bottom of that page) the central figure is an Ox skull. An Ox skull like this was also a symbol used by Whitney. The poem seems to be an elegy to Truth, now deceased and in heaven. If you recognize that a diversionary gender switch is being played , which is fitting considering the comic theme of so many of the plays, it is easy to see this emblem as an answer to the "Wounded Truth" of the Quarto emblems.

A BEAVTEOVS maide, in comly wise doth stand:
Who on the Sunnes bright globe, doth cast her eie:
An opened booke, she holdeth in her hand,
withall the Palme, in signe of victorie;
 · Her right foote treadeth downe the world belowe:
Her name is T R V T H, of old depainted so .

Her nakednes beseemes simplicitie:
The Sunne, how she is greatest frend to light:
Her booke, the strength she holds by * historie:
The Palme, her triumphes over Tyrants spite:
 The world she treads on, how in heaven she dwels,
 · And here beneath all earthly thing excells .

Historia-custos
illustrium viro-
rum virtutis, testi-
is malorum scele-
ris, beneficia in
omnes humanum
Genus: Diodorus
Siculus. 1. Sobla-
thes 2

V i.

**Truth emblem,** page from *Minerva Britanna.*

## *Taming of A Shrew*  Q1

*Taming of A Shrew* Q1 was printed in 1594 by Peter Short for
Cuthbert Burby. The play is anonymous, and has never been
officially accepted or folded in to the Shakespeare Canon.
The standard story is that "Shakespeare" re-wrote this old
play *The Taming of a Shrew* and transformed it into his play
*The Taming of The Shrew*.  At some point in the future, the
facts will emerge that de Vere wrote both the source play *and*
the final version of *Shrew*.  This is one of the four plays,

believed to have been written by Oxford, and performed by the troupe of his friend the Earl of Pembroke.

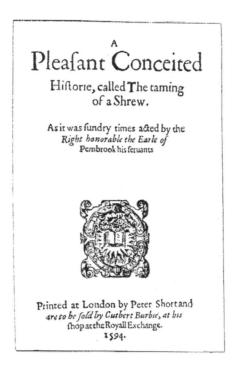

*Taming of <u>a</u> Shrew*, title page.

The emblem used on this quarto, once again filling space where the name of the author might go, is another fascinating puzzle (see enlargement next page). Portrayed is a Blazing Book, descending from Heaven. The Inscription as displayed, with words broken up, is:

ET  VS  QVEAD  NV BES  VERIT  AS  TVA

This should be read in clear Latin as :

ET USQUE  AD  NUBES VERITAS  TUA

| | | |
|---|---|---|
| Et | = | "And" |
| Usque | = | "even to ... " , "Always" , "Even Until" |
| Ad | = | "To", "Towards" , or "Next to" |
| Nubes | = | "Clouds" "Obscurations" ", or "Veils" |
| Veritas Tua | = | "Your TRUTH" |

131

Read literally:      "And your Truth extends even to the Clouds"
Read more freely:  "**And your Truth is, until (then), Obscured**"

**Blazing book emblem** from *Taming of a Shrew*.

The inscription is divided into four sectors. In the lower left quadrant we find the partial words: "BES VERIT". Several anagrams can be created with these letters, the most blatant being: "It be Ver's" or if you prefer, "It B Vere's". One curious fact I must also mention is that the word "Bes" has a specific meaning in Latin. It means "two thirds". Now admittedly, the math doesn't quite add up, but "two-thirds of VERIT" is "VER", give or take a little of the " I ".

I don't question the fact that this emblem is "Peter Shorts Device". The initials P. and S. appear at the bottom of the emblem, left and right.

This Blazing Book emblem is identified by McKerrow as #278. He cites a first use by Short in 1592 on the cover of *A Plaine Discoverie of ten English Lepers, verie noisome and hurtfull to the Church and common wealth...*, Published by Thomas Timme, Minister. This book belongs in the War of Words category. It is well printed, with special woodcuts throughout. The dedication inside is to William Brooke, Baron Cobham. The ten "lepers" are: Schismatics, Church-robbers, Simoniacs, Hypocrites, Proud Men, Gluttons, Fornicators, Covetous Men, Murderers, and Murmurers.

My reading of the Motto as " Et usque ad Nubes Veritas Tua " was confirmed when I found the older, source emblem in Whitney. In Whitney's *Choice of Emblemes*, 1586, the device is called "**Veritas invicta**", which means "Truth Invincible". In this emblem, the Book descends on wings from Heaven, and the Devil below tries to pull it down with a chain. This gruesome detail is absent from the later emblem used by Peter Short. Here the motto "Et Usque Ad Nubes Veritas Tua" is written directly on the book.

### *Henry the Sixth, Part 3* Q1

*Henry the Sixth, Part 3* Q1 was first published in 1595. The quarto was printed by Peter Short for Thomas Millington. Once again, an Anonymous author and an archaic text. Standard scholars call this a "bad" quarto.

The full title as given is: *The True Tragedie of Richard Duke of Yorke, and the death of good King Henrie the Sixth, with the whole contention between the two Houses Lancaster and Yorke, as it was sundrie times acted by the Right Honorable the Earle of Pembrooke his Servants.*

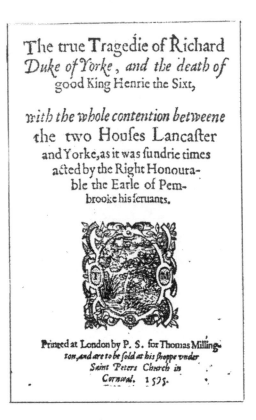

The true Tragedie of Richard
Duke of Yorke, and the death of
good King Henrie the Sixt,

with the whole contention betweene
the two Houfes Lancafter
and Yorke, as it was fundrie times
acted by the Right Honourable the Earle of Pem-
brooke his feruants.

Printed at London by P. S. for Thomas Milling-
ton, and are to be fold at his fhoppe vnder
Saint Peters Church in
Cornwal. 1595.

*Henry VI* **Q1**, title page.

Henry Herbert, the 2$^{nd}$ Earl of Pembroke (c. 1534 - 1601) was a wealthy and influential peer. He married Mary Sidney, the poet's sister, and she became the famous Countess of Pembroke by his hand. Their children were William and Philip Herbert, the later Earls of Pembroke and Montgomery who are the dedicatees of the *First Folio* of Shakespeare.

Henry Herbert's connections to the 17$^{th}$ Earl of Oxford are numerous. From their sitting together in judgment at the trial of Mary Queen of Scots (1587) to the negotiations for the marriage of Oxford's daughter Bridget Vere to William Herbert (Henry's son) in 1597. (They did not get married, but his brother Philip Herbert, the Earl of Montgomery, co-patron of the Shakespeare *First Folio* was married to Oxford's daughter, Susan Vere.)

Like several of the Earls, Henry Herbert kept a dramatic troupe. There are records that they toured in the country in the 1570's and 80's, but did not make a splash or impression at Court or the London stage until the early 1590's. Pembroke's Men played *Edward II* (attributed to Marlowe) and *Taming of A Shrew*, the anonymous source of the later "Shakespeare" play. They played *The First Part of the Contention, Titus Andronicus*, and *The True Tragedie* ... the work under discussion. The prevailing theory is that having played these works, an agent of Pembroke's men sold the four texts to Millington and Burby, who farmed them out to printers.

Why would Oxford's anonymous plays be used by his friend's troupe and not his own? Perhaps because Oxford's Men and Oxford's Boys, which had been active throughout the 1580's went quiet in the early 1590's, just as Pembroke's men were taking off (with their new material). Oxford's first wife Anne died in 1588, the same year as the Spanish Armada. In the aftermath of the war, and the loss of his wife, Oxford changed gears. Then he remarried, and went somewhat into retirement to write, and curtailed his former hobby of producing theatrical events more directly. Oxford's Troupe was revived in the last few years of his life, and he was granted a special license by the Queen to produce plays.

The emblem on *The True Tragedy*, shown on the next page, is considered to be Millington's because it has his initials T. M. It shows a tree, bent over; blown by gusty wind, but withstanding the pressure.

Then, in your waies let reafon ftrike the ftroke,
ASPASIA fhonne, althoughe her face doe fhine :
But, if you like of HYMENÆVS yoke,
PENELOPE preferre, thoughe fpinninge twine,
Yet if you like, how moft to liue in reft,
HIPPOLYTVS his life, fuppofe the beft.

*Vincit qui patitur.*

THE mightie oke, that fhrinkes not with a blafte,
But ftiflie ftandes, when Boreas mofte doth blowe,
With rage thereof, is broken downe at lafte,
When bending reedes, that couche in tempeftes lowe
  With yeelding ftill, doe fafe, and founde appeare :
  And looke alofte, when that the cloudes be cleare.

*Erafm. in Epift.*
*Verè magni ani-*
*mi eft, quafdam*
*iniurias neglige-*
*re, nec ad quo-*
*rundam conutci*
*aures, vel lin-*
*guam habere.*

When Enuie, Hate, Contempte, and Slaunder, rage :
Which are the ftormes, and tempeftes, of this life ;
With patience then, wee muft the combat wage,
And not with force refift their deadlie ftrife
  But fuffer ftill, and then wee fhall in fine,
  Our foes fubdue, when they with fhame fhall pine.

**Page from** *Henry VI Part 3,* **Q1,** showing Tree emblem. Note footnote in lower left margin.

McKerrow identifies this as emblem # 302. He cites its first use on this very quarto: *The True Tragedy,* 1595. This emblem is also based on a Whitney illustration and poem. The

Whitney emblem, called *Vincit qui patitur* (He who is patient, prevails), identifies the tree as an Oak, and the wind as Boreas. The second stanza of the poem begins:

Which Envy, Hate, Contempt, and Slander rage
Which are the storms, and tempests of this life
With patience then we must the combat wage
And not with force resist their deadly strife.

A margin footnote associated with this verse begins:

Erasmus in Epistles: **Vere magni animi est**, …

Which I presume, in context, means : "The great Truth of life is …"

In any event, the 1595 printer's device echoes the 1586 emblem joined to a conspicuous Vere footnote. I am not suggesting that anything was meant in 1586, but that 9 years later a coy reference was made … perhaps.

There is an interesting "cipher" or word game, suggested by the peculiar typesetting of the title page of *The True Tragedy*, which appears to create an authorial cipher. The printer has made an eccentric decision to use a type size and spacing that "forces" him to split up the words "Honourable" and "Pembrooke" with hyphens, thus creating two odd choppy last lines:

acted by the Right Honoura-
    **ble** the Earle of Pem-
        **brooke** his servants.

Pronounce "ble" as "bull" … as in "honoura**ble**"
A "ble" is a bull, which suggests **Ox**
A "brooke" suggests **Ford**

One of Oxford's titles was Lord Bulbeck. A Bul-Bec is the same as a Bull-Brooke or an Ox-Ford.

One can also read, by reading the first three words of the last three lines, in a zig-zag fashion:

Acted by the Right / Earle the **ble** / **brooke** his servants.

A reprint of this play appeared 5 years later. When the *True Tragedie of Richard Duke of Yorke* was republished by Millington in 1600, someone cleaned up the blurb typesetting, and the "puzzle" if it was one, was removed. But the play remained anonymous.

*True Tragedie* was printed anonymously both in 1595 and 1600. Standard scholars have only gradually and grudgingly accepted this work, and only in the context of its being a "very bad" Shakespeare printing of *H6 part 3*. The alternative for them is to admit that their version of "the Bard" plagiarized wholesale the work of numerous anonymous dramatists. The same problem exists for *Richard III, King John, King Lear, Henry the Fifth, Hamlet, Shrew*, and others. With Oxford as the author, there is no problem with the appearance of so many older, "unpolished" versions of the canonical plays being performed and alluded to when Willem' Shaksper was still a wee laddie in the countrie.

### The Tragedy of King Richard the Second  Q1

The *Tragedy of King Richard the Second*, Q1 was printed in 1597. As shown on the next page, the play again is Anonymous.  The printer was Valentine Simmes and the publisher Andrew Wise. The blurb under the title says :

**As** it hath beene publikely acted
**by** the right Honourable the
**Lorde** Chamberlaine his Servants.

The way the text for this blurb is laid out, one can read vertically (straight down ): "**As** ... **by** ... **Lorde** ... v ("v" being the first letter in "vants"). Oxford was the Lord Great Chamberlain of England. From 1585 to 1596, the Lord Chamberlain of the Household, who had legal authority over all theatrical activities, was Oxford's friend Henry Carey, the Lord Hunsdon. Henry died July 22, 1596, and his office was supposed to go to his son George. But due to politics, the job went to a rival, William Lord Cobham. Cobham held the post for only seven months. He died on

March 5, 1597. George Carey, 2<sup>nd</sup> Lord Hunsdon, became Lord Chamberlain on March 17, 1597. All very neat and tidy. *The Tragedie of King Richard the Second* was registered at the Stationers' on Aug. 29, 1597. There were no "Shakespeare" registrations while Cobham was briefly on the job.

*Richard II* **title pages.** Left: Q1, right: Q2.

The emblem on *Richard II* Q1, shown next page, shows a man with his left arm weighted down and his right hand touching a cloud of heaven. The man also has wings on his arms. There is a village in the background and a man waving from a cloud (perhaps meant to be God). Because this man is stuck in the middle, I am tempted to call this the "Middleman" emblem. There is no Latin inscription.

**"Middleman" emblem.** Enlarged from *Richard II* Q1 title page.

McKerrow provides some useful information on this emblem, which in his book is #142. His description is : "A boy with wings upon his right arm and with his left hand holding, or fastened to, a weight." He adds that the emblem is derived from an Alciati emblem signifying "talent kept from rising by the burden of poverty". The design elements of this emblem were used by several printers on the Continent and England in the 1560's-70's. McKerrow states that the woodcut for this emblem dates as far back as 1563 in England. Its use can be traced to 1571, but then it seemed to lay "fallow" for 26 years. Somehow the emblem was "resurrected" by Valentine Simmes in 1597. And what was his first use for this antique emblem? *The Tragedie of King Richard the Second* Q1, anonymous, as described above.

In 1598, Valentine Simmes brought out a second edition of *Richard II*, the Q2. The text is virtually identical to Q1. Both plays contain a "deposition scene" but not the full scene where Richard II surrenders his crown. Those lines were first "restored" into the printed text in the Q4 of 1608.

The 1598 Q2 also uses the Middleman emblem. The descriptive blurb has been reset with the result that the vertical cryptogram on Q1 (if that's what it was) is gone. But there is an even more crucial difference. An author's credit has been added : "By William Shake-speare".

Oxfordian theory suggests that for one reason or another, perhaps because of the "Isle of Dogs" fiasco, the "heat came down" on Lord Oxford by his political friends and enemies to disassociate himself from his theatrical activities. It is likely that in 1598 the use of the "Shake-speare" pseudonym began to be enforced.

It is also significant that the Middleman Emblem, once acquired by Simmes, (or Andrew Wise, the publisher) did not become his principal or trademark emblem. It does not appear on the majority of his productions. McKerrow mentions only a few post - *Richard II* uses of "Middleman" by Simmes.

I've found several more. The principal follow-up uses are :

* *Pasquil's Mad-Cap and his Message*, 1600 (Anonymous, but attributed to Nicholas Breton)

This is a peculiar little book in the Pasquil mythos (presumably started by Oxford and/or Nashe around 1589 in the anti-Martin pamphlets ).

* *The Shoemakers Holiday*, 1600, Anon. (always attributed later to Thomas Dekker)

* *The Tragicall History of Doctor Faustus*, Q1, 1604, by Christopher Marlowe. Marlowe had been dead for about 11 years when this play was finally printed. One wonders if the publication of this controversial play has anything to do with Oxford's death in 1604, and papers escaping.

So the evidence suggests that someone had access to an antique emblem and gave it to Valentine Simmes to use on certain books. The first such book was the anonymous (but not for long) *Richard II* in 1597.

*The Tragedy of King Richard the Third* Q1 was published in 1597. It was printed by Valentine Simmes for Andrew Wise. The play is anonymous, and is stated to be the script of the production used by the Lord Chamberlain's Men. The quarto was registered on Oct. 20, 1597.

This publication's title page (shown on the next page), has two stylized block prints, not described by McKerrow. The Header emblem features a winged goddess flanked by two griffins. The lower blockprint also shows a winged-face, with scroll work and two roses.

One of the Vere heraldic emblems is a Bird with a human female face, below: sometimes described as a Harpy, elsewhere as an Eagle with an Angel's face.

**Vere heraldic emblem.**

# THE TRAGEDY OF
## King Richard the third.

### Containing,
His treacherous Plots againſt his brother Clarence:
the pittiefull murther of his iunocent nephewes:
his tyrannicall vſurpation : with the whole courſe
of his deteſted life, and moſt deſerued death.

### As it hath beene lately Acted by the
Right honourable the Lord Chamberlaine his ſeruants.

### AT LONDON
¶ Printed by Valentine Sims, for Andrew Wiſe,
dwelling in Paules Chuch-yard, at the
Signe of the Angell.
1597.

*Richard III*, Q1, title page.

The original mythical harpies of ancient Greece differed,
having bat-wings and tiger-claws. A Harpy in Heraldry is
usually described as a creature with the wings and body of a

143

vulture combined with the head, neck, and breasts of a woman.

In *The Tempest*, the climax of Act III features a wild dance by Ariel in the form of a Harpy. Shakespeare has occasion to describe a harpy in the play *Pericles*.

CLEON:      Thou art like the **harpy**,
            Which, to betray, dost, **with thine angel's face**,
            **Seize with thine eagle's talons**.
            *Pericles* Act 4, Scene 3

### Romeo and Juliet Q1

John Danter printed and sold this first quarto of the world famous play. Its original title was: *An Excellent conceited Tragedie of Romeo and Juliet*. The text seems severely flawed, compared to the later text we are accustomed to, but it is not clear what exactly Danter was working from. The "bad" quarto label does not really fit this *Romeo & Juliet* text, because scholars agree that Danter's version has sections that are better than the revised edition. The "flawed" first quarto has more stage directions intact than the corrected version. So Danter may have had a script from an archaic version of the play.

The principal device is the emblem on the title page variously called "Opportunity" or "Occasion" or "Fortune". Danter's woodcut device features the innovation "Aut Nunci Aut Nunquam", Now or **Never**, which has been described on pages 135-136 of this book.

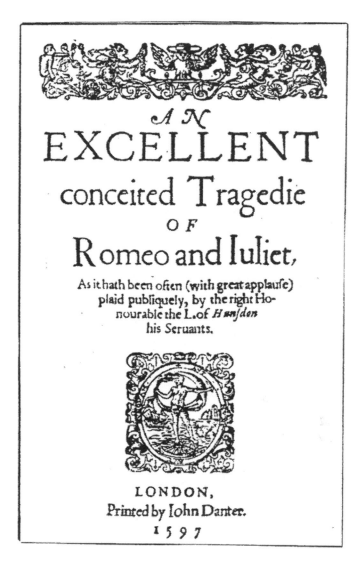

*Romeo & Juliet*, Q1, title page.

*Fortune* is one of the main themes in *Romeo & Juliet*, as the heroine herself explains:

Juliet:        O Fortune, Fortune! all men call thee fickle.
                     If thou art fickle, what dost thou with him

145

That is renown'd for faith? Be fickle, Fortune,
For then I hope thou wilt not keep him long
But send him back.
*R&J* Act III, Scene 5

The interesting extra feature of the *R&J* Q1 title page is the comical headpiece at the top.

Central in this image is an Owl, with a hat on. The owl is perched on a raised bar, and creatures to its left and right seem to be offering presents (pearls or grapes perhaps). An Owl represents wisdom, and secrecy. Owls fly at night, stealthily. The owl's screech has a penetrating terror. An owl "with a hat on" may represent a extra level of secrecy... as in: "keep this under your hat ". The Owl also represents the Goddess Pallas Athene, as well as her Roman counterpart, Minerva.

Pallas Athene/Minerva also has the epithet "Hasti Vibrans" which means "Spear-Shaker". Pallas Athene was a warrior, and the patron of Drama as well. It has been argued well, in other works which investigate the Oxford hypothesis fairly, that Edward de Vere's choice of the pseudonym "Shake-Speare" was primarily an allusion to Athene/Minerva. Athena also wore a goatskin, and the Greek word for goat (Tragos) gave us the word "Tragedy", literally "the Goat-song". Unfortunately (for the goat) the "song of the goat" was the yelp of its own sacrificial demise.

### Henry the Fourth, Part 1 Q1

*Henry the Fourth*, Part 1 Q1 was first published in 1598. The printer was Peter Short, and the publisher Andrew Wise. There are two variant editions of this quarto, with different spellings and layout on the title page. The version shown is STC# 22280.

This is a "Good" Quarto. No author is named. Standard scholars have only wispy explanations for why the anonymous "good Quartos" do not credit "William Shaksper" if the man was really a hungry up-and-coming author. Instead of naming the author, Short has pulled out his Blazing Book emblem again:

Et Usque Ad Nubes **Ver**itas Tua:

Until then, **thy Truth is obscured**

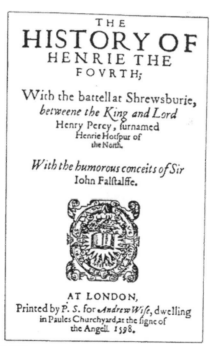

*Henry IV Part 1*, Q1 title page.

## Later quartos of *Romeo & Juliet*

The "corrected, augmented and amended' second quarto of *Romeo & Juliet* was printed by Thomas Creede for Cuthbert Burby in 1598. It was Anonymous.

*Romeo & Juliet* remained an anonymous work until just before it was "established" as Shakespeare's by its inclusion in the *First Folio* of 1623. Though Meres named *R&J* as a Shakespeare play in 1598, the printers and publishers of the popular love tragedy never "cashed in" on the Shakespeare name until the end of 1622.

| | | | | | |
|---|---|---|---|---|---|
| Romeo and Juliet | Q1 | 1597 | Bad | John Danter | (& E. Allde?) |
| Romeo and Juliet | Q2 | 1599 | Good | Creed for | Burby |
| Romeo and Juliet | Q3 | 1609 | Good | Windet for | Smethwicke |
| Romeo and Juliet | Q4 | 1622 | Good | Stansby for | Smethwicke |

At some point after (or during) the publication of the *R&J* Q4 in 1622, Smethwicke must have changed his mind and decided to "cash in". For the Q5 of *Romeo & Juliet* is a variant of the Q4, with the telling difference being the addition of a line to the title page: Written by W. Shake-speare. Standard studies of *Romeo and Juliet* gloss over these problems. They claim that the Q4 is un-datable, and that the non-anonymous version is the intended one. But the modern editions of the Short Title Catalog cleans up these problems and leads to the inference that the commercial value of the name Shakespeare on a book waxed and waned.

**John Smethwicke**, publisher and bookseller, became a freeman of the Stationers' in 1597. In 1607, the copyrights belonging to Nicholas Ling passed to Smethwicke. These included *Loves Labors Lost, Hamlet,* and *Romeo & Juliet.* How could Smethwicke not know *R&J* was by "Shakespeare"?

In 1622 Smethwicke was brought on board as one of the partners of Jaggard in the *First Folio* project. He apparently had to be admitted into the venture because he owned three of the crucial plays. It is at that moment that Smethwicke probably became aware of the commercial cachet of the

Shakespeare brand-name. Smethwicke, in the beginning of his career had been fined repeatedly for publishing "privileged" books. That is, books owned under the copyright of other printers or publishers. After the *Folio*, Smethwicke became the consummate team player. He worked his way up to Junior Warden of the Stationers Company in 1631. He was Senior Warden by 1635, and finally, Master of the Company in 1639. Smethwicke was one of the co-publishers of the *Second Folio* of Shakespeare in 1632.

# Chapter Eleven

# The Quartos, 1598 – 1604

## Loves Labors Lost

Loves Labors Lost appeared in 1598. This is a Q1 "Good" Quarto. The printer was William White, and the publisher again was Cuthbert Burby. This is one of the five "Shakespeare corrected quartos".

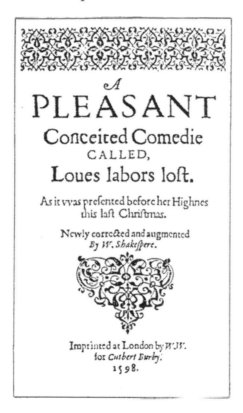

*Loves Labors Lost,* Q1, title page.

In this presentation we have been proceeding chronologically. Including *Taming of a Shrew*, there were **eight** Anonymous plays in a row, printed over four years, that would only later be ascribed to Shakespeare. *Loves*

*Labors Lost* represents the fulcrum point. There would still be more anonymous quartos, but as a rule, "Shakespeare" plays began to be attributed to Shakespeare, from 1598 on. *Loves Labors Lost* gives the credit: "By W. Shakespere."

**William White** got his start in 1597 by taking over the operations of the shop of Richard Jones, who was still alive, but apparently too old or sick to do the actual work anymore. Richard Jones had an illustrious career as a publisher, seller and printer going all the way back to 1564. He printed the play *Damon & Pithias*, both in 1571, and 1582. This play is credited to "Master Edwards", which in standard bibliography refers to Richard Edwards, who is also credited as the editor of the Oxford-drenched *Paradyse of Dainty devises*. Recent scholarship, including my own, identifies *Damon & Pithias* as one of the Earl of Oxford's plays, most likely written while he was still a student at Cambridge. The prologue to *Damon & Pithias* begins:

> On everie side whereas I glaunce my roving eye
> Silence in all eares bent, I plainly do espy.

The concluding couplet:

> Whose upright judgment we do crave, with heedful ear and eye,
> To hear the cause, and see the effect of this new Tragicall Comedie

The author of *Damon & Pithias* seems to have originated a concept, a Tragical Comedie, that is usually credited as Shakespeare's innovation. The Earl of Oxford's authorship addresses this conundrum as well. Richard Jones provides the paper trail confirmation. Jones was the publisher of no less than seven Oxford-related or Oxford-sponsored editions:

| Work | Year | Printer/Publisher | Relevance |
|------|------|-------------------|-----------|
| *The Breviary of Britain* | 1573 | Twyne/Jones | Dedicated to Oxford |
| *Paradyse of Dainty Devises* Q1 | 1576 | Jones/Disle | Poems by Oxford |
| *Paradyse of Dainty Devises* Q2 | 1578 | Jones/Disle | Poems by Oxford |
| *Britton's Bowre of delights* | 1591 | Jones | Poems by Oxford |
| *The English Secretary* Q1 | 1586 | Daye/Jones | Dedicated to Oxford |
| *The English Secretary* Q2 | 1592 | Daye/Jones | Dedicated to Oxford |
| *The English Secretary* Q3 | 1595 | Jones/ Burby | Dedicated to Oxford |

(Angel Daye was Oxford's secretary.)

William White was operating out of Jones' shop when he printed *Love's Labors Lost*, and his later "Shakespeare" projects. His path to authentic manuscripts is made clearer by his involvement with Jones.

On this unique title page of *Loves Labors Lost* are two abstract devices, but no "mythic emblems".

The triangular or heart-shaped woodcut was used occasionally but not habitually by the printer William White. His "regular" emblem shows a pelican biting its chest. So far I have only come across one other publication with the heart-shaped scroll work. It is the Q2 of *The True Tragedie of Richard Duke of Yorke*, 1600. (*Henry Sixth part 3*).

On both these publications White used the heart woodcut in tandem with a flower print pattern block as a header or banner. Note that the Headpiece on *Loves Labors Lost*, is a precise block print repeating the same image horizontally. It is clearly a **floral abstraction with interlaced** V 's. This block print was widely used in Elizabethan era books, so any particular claim as to its original significance would be foolhardy. Nevertheless, this exact floral block print was used so frequently on books that were dedicated to Edward de Vere, that the motif can be easily associated with Oxford's publishing ventures.

The examples shown on these pages are telling because the banner is used directly in association with the dedication page to Oxford.

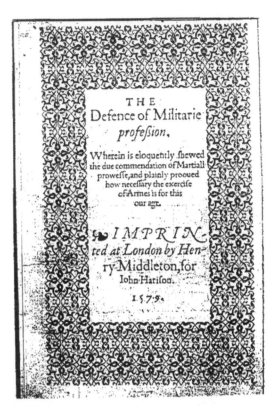

THE
Defence of Militarie
profeſſion,

Wherein is eloquently ſhewed
the due commendation of Martiall
prowesſe, and plainly prooued
how neceſſary the exerciſe
of Armes is for this
our age.

IMPRIN-
ted at London by Hen-
ry Middleton, for
Iohn Hariſon.
1579.

¶ TO THE RIGHT
honorable, *Edward de Vere*, Earle of
Oxenford, vicount Bulbecke, Lord of Eſcales
and Baldeſmere, and Lord great Chamberlaine of England.

*The Defense of the Military Profession*, title page (top) and dedication to Edward de Vere (bottom), both showing floral "V" motif.

*The Defense of the Military Profession*, 1579, by Geffrey Gates was printed by Henry Middleton for John Harrison. It is dedicated to Oxford and bears the full page bookplate of the Vere Arms. This book was a one shot; it was never reprinted. Gates himself was a one-hit wonder, with no other books to his name. The work was a plea to England to develop a standing army, along the lines of the ancient Roman Empire, to infuse culture with discipline, and to be ready, at all times, to ward off invaders, rather than raise an army, as needed, which was the current protocol in England. Lord Oxford was pleading to the Queen for a major military assignment in the same time frame as the appearance of this book. The significance of all this is that there are echoes of *Defense of the Military Profession* in the Shakespeare play *Timon of Athens*. Oxford's political philosophy, as expressed by Gates is also present in the strident nationalistic fervor of the Shakespeare History plays. In addition, the publisher of *Defense*, John Harrison, was the same man who 14 years later was entrusted to publish *Venus & Adonis*, and *The Rape of Lucrece*, the Shakespeare poems.

*Zelauto*, 1580, was only printed once. It is a lavish prduction with illustrations, all masterminded by Oxford, and his assistant at the time, Anthony Munday. The printer was John Charlewood. Here the dedication page to Oxford is once again graced with the V-block print.

John Charlewood was a major player in Elizabethan publishing. He was a printer, a bookseller, and a publisher at various times in his long career. Originally in the Grocers' guild, he was transferered to the Stationers' Company in 1574. In 1579 Charlewood and Richard Jones purchased 15 book copyrights from Henry Denham. All three men published books for the Earl of Oxford. By 1583 he was in trouble for regularly printing books under copyright to others. Charlewood won the exclusive right to print playbills for the theaters in 1587. Charlewood was involved in the religious "war of words" and is mentioned by the mysterious Martin Marprelate in his tracts. When Charlewood died in 1593, there was a fight to obtain the lucrative playbill monopoly between William Jaggard and James Roberts.

Roberts won the contract when he married Alice Charlewood, the publisher's widow.

*Zelauto* title page and dedication.

The significance of *Zelauto* is threefold.

1. The book is acknowledged by all commentators to have been used by "Shakespeare" when he was writing the subplots of *The Merchant of Venice*.

2. The book *Zelauto* was written by Anthony Munday while he was in the service of the Earl of Oxford. It says so right on the title page. Considering that Oxford's method of writing stories seems to have consisted of speaking extemporaneously while a secretary scribbled it all down, the actual author of *Zelauto* is likely to be Oxford himself. Another Oxford secretary, Angel Daye, streamlined available shorthand methods, probably in an effort to keep up with his rapidly speaking employer. His book *The English Secretary*, also dedicated to Oxford, offers insight into the methods that may have been used by the eccentric genius who was the actual author of the Shakespeare plays.

3. The printer of *Zelauto,* John Charlewood, was in business with other Oxford-related printers, and a portion of his stock and copyrights ended up in the hands of James Roberts, who was connected to Oxford, and an important owner and printer of "Shakespeare" manuscripts.

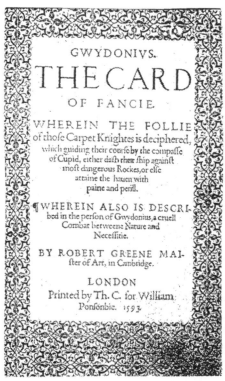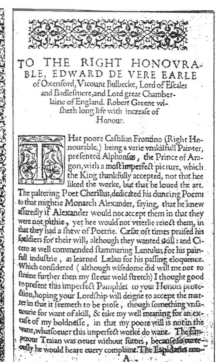

*Gwydonius Card of Fancie,* title page and dedication.

*Gwydonius Carde of Fancy,* 1593, Q3, was a new issue of the book by Robert Greene, which was first published in 1584. In all three editions the book carried its dedication to Edward de Vere. The 1593 printing by Thomas Creede was the first book he ever printed under his own name. This is discussed futher at page 94. In the 1593 edition the dedication to Oxford has the same V-block design used on *Defense* and *Zelauto.* The same design appears on *Loves Labors Lost,* in my view, acting as a counterbalance to the first title page attribution of a play to the name William Shakespeare.

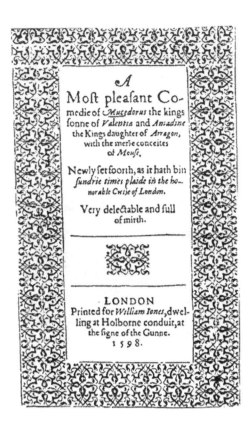

*Mucedorus*, title page.

In the same year, 1598, a quarto was published of a play called *Mucedorus*. William White was the printer, though he left his name off the first edition. This play is classified as Shakespearean Apocrypha. The authorship of this Q1, 1598, has been hotly debated. Note that the same " V - Block print " used on *Loves Labors Lost* surrounds the page. More significant is that between the two horizontal lines is a kind of sigil made by turning the V - block on its side. As this design motif had already been associated with Oxford's name in books, it is rather telling that William White chose it to place *between the lines*, where the author's name should be.

Note also that above the author's 'sigil' is the statement "Very delectable and full of mirth."

"Ver y de lectable" can be re-arranged to cipher "ylect a ble, de Ver" . < elect a Bull, de Ver >

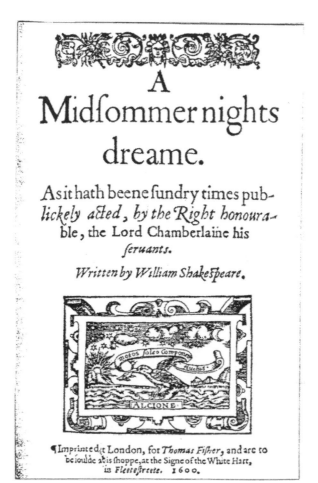

*A Midsummer Nights Dream*, Q1, title page.

## A Midsommer nights dreame

"*A Midsommer nights dreame*" first appeared in Quarto in 1600. This is a Q1, "Good" quarto. The name of the printer is not given, but the *Short Title* editors think it was Richard Bradocke, who had printed Marlowe's *Edward II*. The publisher-seller, Thomas Fisher, is also something of a cipher. He was not involved in any other Shakespeare material. Moreover, Fisher was only in business from 1600 -

1602, and only published four books, his entire career output.

The play A *Midsummer Nights Dream*, is thought to have premiered at the wedding, in 1595, of William Stanley, the 6th Earl of Derby, and his bride Elizabeth de Vere, Oxford's eldest daughter. Several orthodox Shakespeare scholars admit that *MND* has that connection to a Vere family event. The publication, in 1600, was well done. Experts think that *Dream* 1600 was one of the best of the good quartos, coming from an authentic working text from the author or acting company.

This title page is distinguished by an ornamental Headpiece and a complex Emblem featuring a kingfisher bird which bears the label "ALCIONE". On this quarto the author is credited as "William Shakespeare", with the spelling that is now familiar. In October, 1600, this was the 12th or 13th Q1 play to appear since 1594. Of the first ten Q1 plays, nine do not name an author. After August, 1600, all the new first quartos credit "Shakespeare", although four variant spellings are used. It appears that use of the name "Shakespeare", either as a brand name, or a pseudonym, was instituted in 1598 and became fully enforced by the summer of 1600.

Now to the Quarto. Below the title, A Midsommer nights dreame, is a blurb stating this play had been acted by "the Lord Chamberlaine his servants". Edward de Vere was, of course, the Lord Great Chamberlain of England, not "the Lord Chamberlain", but the use of the cliché seems to play into the covert "signatures" we have been discussing. The capitalized word "Right" placed directly over "Chamberlaine" is suggestive, because "right" is etymologically related to the word "great".

Note also that the way the type is set, "honourable" is split with a hyphen, (a gimmick used on *The True Tragedy*, 1595) and thus the next line reads:

ble, the Lord Chamberlain ...

Pronounced just like the "ble" in "honourable", we have:

Bull, the Lord Chamberlain.

A Bull of course, is just a knife stroke away from being an Ox.

**Alcione emblem** from title page of *Midsommer Nights Dream,* Q1.

Now let us look more closely at the Emblem on the title page of *A Midsommer nights dreame*. This rectangular emblem shows a Kingfisher bird atop the ocean with a fish in its mouth, the Sun setting over a distant island, and the stars and Moon out overhead. In addition there is a banner with the Latin Inscription: Motos Soleo Componere Fluctus.

The label ALCIONE refers the reader back to Greek mythology. There were two different Alcyones, and they are both indicated in this emblem.

One Alcyone was a nymph, who was one of the Seven Sisters of the Pleiades constellation. The Pleiades, visible with the naked eye, are in the constellation Taurus, the Bull. These are the stars which seem to be depicted in the emblem: the Pleiades and Taurus.

The birthdate that we have for Edward de Vere, is April 12, 1550, old-style. The astronomical date corresponds to April 22. Thus we learn that the 17th Earl of Oxford was probably a Taurus. Astrological Taurus is a symbol of the Ox as well as the Bull. Apis the Ox, the Egyptian herald of the Gods, was an image known to de Vere from *Ovid's Metamorphoses*. Nashe referred to Oxford in "Strange Newes" as "Apis Lapis", one interpretation of which is "stoned Ox" (a "de-masculinized" bull). Shakespeare asks:

"Were we not born under Taurus ?" *Twelfth Night* , Act I, scene 3

In Astrology, the ancient "Ruler" of Taurus is Venus, Oxford's favorite inspiration. The mythological connection between Venus and Taurus goes back almost 3000 years. One possible reason is that Venus, when passing through its phases, appears in sharp crescent shapes as seen from Earth. Before pollution and electric lights ruined humans' night vision, it is believed that people could see the "Horns" of Venus with the naked eye. And our ancestors made a connection between the horns of Venus and the horns of Taurus, and with the horns of the crescent Moon. The crescent Moon can be seen in the upper right of the Alcione emblem.

The more famous Alcione appears in the myth of Ceyx and Alcione which first came to England in Book 11 of *Ovid's Metamorphoses*. Ceyx was the mortal son of Hesperus, the Evening Star, otherwise known as the planet Venus. It is not clear if Greek and Roman astronomers and storytellers really understood the complexities of Venus' orbit. Venus appears in the morning for 221 days, then disappears for a while, and reappears as the Evening star for 221 days. At various times it was believed that two different gods were involved. So Venus, Goddess of Love and Beauty, does not always correspond to myths that refer to Venus the planet, or to Hesperus, the Evening Star.

Ceyx (whose name in English sounds like "sex") married Alcione, a mortal woman. In one story, they were so taken with their own grandeur that they imagined themselves to rival Zeus and Hera. In punishment, they were turned into birds. In a slightly different myth, Alcione grieves alone at home, believing falsely that her husband Ceyx has died in a shipwreck. Despondent, she flings herself into the Sea. She is miraculously saved from drowning when the Goddess Thetis turns her, and her husband, into Halcyon birds. The Halcyon is the Kingfisher. Halcyons were believed to have the power to calm the winds and still the raging seas. This myth is the origin of our phrase "halcyon days" which means "the good old days when things were peaceful" or "springtime".

Shakespeare used the phrase:

PUCELLE:    Assign'd am I to be the English scourge.
            This night the siege assuredly I'll raise.
            Expect Saint Martin's summer, halcyon days
            *Henry the Sixth, Part 1* Act I. Scene 2


And now we come to the smoking gun. Two published book dedications to Oxford make references to Alcione, decades before the 1600 emblem.

In 1571, Arthur Golding's translation of the *Psalms of David* was published. It was printed by Thomas East and Henry Middleton for the sellers Lucas Harrison, and George Byshop. The book contains a long dedication to Goldings' nephew and former star student, Edward de Vere, who had just turned 21, and taken his seat in Parliament for the first time. The dedication to Oxford, dated October 20, 1571, has a mildly patronizing tone; his uncle exhorting him to avoid vice and wickedness, and devote himself to the study of God's word, and commandments. The book appeared around the time of Oxford's marriage to Anne Cecil, which occurred in December 1571. The final paragraph of Golding's statement alludes to Oxford's marriage to Anne, and the influence that being a son-in-law to Lord Burghley might have on his career:

...To the furtherance whereof, God hath by household alliance linked unto your Lordship a long-experienced Nestor, whose counsel and footsteps if you follow, no doubt but you shall be both happy in yourself, and singularly profitable to your commonwealth; and moreover, God shall bless you with plentiful and godly issue by your vertuous and dear-beloved spouse, to continue the honor and renown of your noble house after the happy knitting up of both your years, which I pray God may be many in unseparable love, *like the love of **Ceyx and Alcyone***, to the glory of God and the contentation of both your desires. Written at London the 20 of October, 1571. Your Lordship's most humble to command, Arthur Golding

Golding, a puritanical Calvinist, exhorts young Oxford to follow a godly Christian path, but uses the language and stories of ancient pagan mythology to pique his interest.

The second example is contained in the dedication by John Lyly to his employer Edward de Vere, in the book *Euphues and His England*, 1580. Lyly was secretary to Oxford from the late 1570's to about 1582, and wrote his intial novels and plays while in service to de Vere. Lyly's first book: *Euphues, the Anatomy of Wit*, came out in 1578. Two years later, in the published sequel, *Euphues and His England*, Lyly thanks Oxford for his continued protection and patronage. Lyly, in describing how the two books got written says:

"I have now finished both my labours, **the one being hatched in the hard winter with the Alcyon**, the other not daring to bud till the cold was past, like the Mulbery, in either of the which or in both, if I seem to glean after another's cart, for a few ears of corn, or of the tailor's shreds to make me a livery, I will not deny, but I am one of those poets, which make the painters fain to come into Homer's basin, there to lap up, that he doth cast up."

The way I understand this statement, Lyly is admitting he has turned anecdotes and stories and tales spun by Oxford, and used them to make the patchwork quilt of the *Euphues* novels.

It is another interesting coincidence that the Mulberry tree, and its blood red fruit, was a favorite symbol of Shakespeare, figuring in the plot and metaphor of both *Venus & Adonis,* and *Midsummer Nights Dream.*

> When he beheld **his shadow in the brook**,
> The fishes spread on it their golden gills;
> When he was by, **the birds** such pleasure took,
> That some would sing, some **other in their bills**
> **Would bring him mulberries** and ripe-red cherries;
> He fed them with his sight, they him with berries.
>
> But this foul, grim, and urchin-snouted **boar**,
> Whose downward eye still looketh for a grave,
> Ne'er saw **the beauteous livery that he wore**;
> Witness the entertainment that he gave:
> If he did see his face, why then I know
> He thought to kiss him, and hath kill'd him so.
>
> 'Tis **true**, 'tis **true**; thus was Adonis slain:
> He ran upon **the boar with his sharp spear**,
> Who did not whet his teeth at him again,
> But by a kiss thought to persuade him there;
> And nuzzling in his flank, the loving swine
> Sheathed unaware the tusk in his soft groin.
>    *Venus & Adonis,* 1593

QUINCE     And as she fled, her mantle she did fall
                  Which Lion vile with bloody mouth did stain.
                  Anon comes Pyramus, sweet youth and tall,
                  And finds his trusty Thisby's mantle slain;
                  Whereat with blade, with bloody blameful blade
                  He bravely broach'd his boiling bloody breast;
                  And Thisby, **tarrying in mulberry shade**
                  **His dagger drew, and died**. For all the rest ...

*Midsummer Nights Dream* Act 5, Scene 1

A classical source of information on the Alcyone, or the Kingfisher bird, is *Pliny's Natural History*. The following quote from Pliny is from Book 10, section 47:

> ... A kingfisher is very rarely seen, and only at the setting of the Pleiades, and about midsummer or midwinter, when it occasionally flies around a ship and at once goes away to its retreat. They breed

at midwinter, on what are called "the kingfisher days", during which the sea is calm and navigable, especially in the neighborhood of Sicily ... They lay five eggs at a time.

And now to the motto: Motos Soleo Componere Fluctus. It might be an apropos motto for the kingfisher bird, or perhaps a bawdy wedding benediction.

Motos       having been moved , now aroused, shaken
Soleo       I am accustomed, It's the usual thing
            (soleo is slang for the sexual "doing it")
Componere  to compose, to calm , to conjoin
Fluctus     the rough (seas) , turbulence , commotion , a tempest (flux)

The conservative Latin translation is:
Moved, I am accustomed to calming the turbulence.

The possible meaning of this phrase, considering its appearance on the title page of this play, *A Midsummer Nights Dream* is:
Aroused, doing it, I calm the commotion.

An extreme poetic alternative is:
Shake'n, as ever, I compose the Tempest.

In McKerrow, the ALCIONE emblem is #321. He states that *Midsummer Nights Dreame* is the First use, and my research concurs. It appears that the emblem was cut specifically to be put on this lavishly printed quarto, and that "Mr. Fisher" was put into the booksellers business at the same time. Two other known uses of this emblem are on the two parts of *Antonio & Mellida* and *Antonio's Revenge* by "I.M.", 1602. These plays are both from the children of Paul's and have arguable links to Oxford. The only other use of this Alcione emblem is on a quarto called "*Pasquil's Mistresse : Or the Worthy and Unworthy Woman ...*", 1600. This book is credited to Nicholas Breton, and with reason : the Dedication Epistle is signed "Salohcin Treboun" which is an anagram of his name. My conjecture that all of the above four books, which bear Fisher's Alcione emblem, relate in some way to the marriage of William Stanley, the 6th Earl of Derby to Elizabeth de Vere, Oxford's eldest and most willfully spirited daughter.

This simple pictograph of a bird, when analyzed, has yielded symbolic representations of Venus and Ver (Springtime), and the Ox, (Taurus). The "V" of Venus and Vere is also **V**, the Roman Numeral for Five. And a five pointed star is not only "The Star of Venus", but is de Vere's own symbol. Take another look at the Vere Arms. During the Crusades, the five-pointed Vere Star was thought to represent the Magi's Star of Bethlehem. Venus is invoked frequently in the action of *A Midsummer Nights Dream*. All Shakespeare plays have Five Acts. The reference to Alcyone ties into allusions to Alcyone, in prior printed dedications to Oxford. Who was the Elizabethan Kingfish?

Although I am identifying what appear to be covert or cryptic "signatures" on these quarto pages, I am not asserting that de Vere directly designed or ordered their placement. If the graphic clues are, in fact, there, and not a product of my imagination, then the likeliest scenario is that the printers themselves used their usual methods to surreptitiously credit the author who could not be directly named. It is also possible of course, that the author, wounded by the politics that demanded his anonymity, couldn't resist providing some of these "signatures" or suggestive emblems.

### Henry the Fourth, Part 2, Q1

*Henry the Fourth, Part 2*, Q1 was printed in 1600 by V. Simmes for Wise and Aspley. This is a "good" quarto, containing a reasonable text of the play. The title page blurb identifies the drama as coming from the company of the Lord Chamberlain. It is credited to *William Shakespeare*, but we have seen that after 1598, this had become a brand-name, and Andrew Wise was one of the first to use it. Recall that the 1597 first quartos of *Richard II* and *Richard III*, both published by Wise, were Anonymous. A year later he republished both plays with the name Shake-speare added. William Aspley was Wise's co-publisher on *Henry the Fourth, Part 2*, Q1, 1600 and *Much Ado about Nothing*, Q1, 1600. Aspley in 1609 published the Sonnets.

The distinctive feature on the title page of *Henry the Fourth, Part 2* is a strange emblem. This unusual device is a stylized V shape, or a Vase, with a hairy face within. This face is easy to identify, as he is common in British folklore. He is the Green Man: the sprouting, omnipresent nature god of the Celts.

In Latin, a "Green Man" could be Viridis Vir , or Virescit Vir. Either translation provides a lovely pun : Viridis Vir sounds like "Vere , it is Vere !" Virescit Vir sounds like "Vere is it !...Vere".

Of course I'm aware that many Elizabethan printers blocks contained designs featuring a Green Man. Its use elsewhere doesn't take away from its specific use here. McKerrow catalogues only a later 17th century Green Man emblem and *seems* to have missed the one used in the 1570's through 1590's.

THE
Second part of Henrie
the fourth, continuing to his death,
and coronation of Henrie
the fift.

With the humours of fir Iohn Fal-
ftaffe, and fwaggering
Piftoll.

As it hath been fundrie times publikely
acted by the right honourable, the Lord
Chamberlaine his feruants.

Written by William Shakefpeare.

LONDON
Printed by V .S.for Andrew Wife,and
William Afpley.
1600.

*Henry IV Part 2*, Q1 title page.

The Green Man used here seems to be the one that I have traced as far back as *Hekatompathia*, 1582, a poetry anthology credited to Thomas Watson that is not only dedicated to Edward de Vere, but standard scholars of Watson have conceded that Vere wrote the witty editorial introductions and comments throughout the book. And here we get into smoking gun territory again. *Hekatompathia, the Passionate Century of Love*, dedicated to Oxford, edited *by* Oxford, and probably paid for by him, is the acknowledged source of plot elements in "Shakespeare's" *Othello* and *Measure for Measure*. *Hekatompathia* is also one of the poetic and stylistic "Sources of Shakespeare". Finally it contains a feast of woodcut emblems, many of which seem (at this point) to be first uses. The *Hekatompathia* quarto features the same Green Man emblem which appears 18 years later on the *Henry the Fourth, Part 2* quarto under discussion. In 1582, the Green Man appears in conjunction with the V-Block print also associated with Edward de Vere publications.

*Hekatompathia*, title page (left), and interior page (right) showing "Green Man" emblem.

# Much adoe about
# Nothing

*As it hath been sundrie times publikely*
acted by,the right honourable,the Lord
Chamberlaine his seruants.

*Written by William Shakespeare.*

**LONDON**
Printed by V.S.for Andrew Wise,and
William Aspley.
1600.

*Much Ado About Nothing,* Q1 title page.

## *Much adoe about Nothing* Q1

*Much adoe about Nothing* Q1 was printed in 1600 by Simmes for Wise, and Aspley. This quarto has much in common with the *Henry IV part 2* quarto just examined. In fact, both books were registered on the same day, August 23, 1600. A strange fact is that on August 4, 1600, there was a prior entry for *Much Ado* which says that the play was to be "stayed", that is, prevented from further publication. Somehow, over the course of 19 days, Andrew Wise (or Simmes, or Aspley) received permission to register *Much Ado* for legal publication. But perhaps they got permission for a one-shot printing only, because unlike the other quartos, *Much Ado* was never reprinted, until the *Folio* of 1623.

Once again the Green Man emblem is displayed.

## The moſt excellent

Hiſtorie of the *Merchant of Venice*.

VVith the extreame crueltie of *Shylocke* the Iewe
towards the ſayd Merchant, in cutting a iuſt pound
of his fleſh : and the obtayning of *Portia*
by the choyſe of three
cheſts.

*As it hath beene diuers times acted by the Lord
Chamberlaine his Seruants.*

Written by William Shakeſpeare.

AT LONDON,
Printed by *I. R.* for Thomas Heyes,
and are to be ſold in Paules Church-yard, at the
ſigne of the Greene Dragon.
·1 6 0 0.

*Merchant of Venice*, Q1 title page.

## *Merchant of Venice*, **Q1**

*Merchant of Venice*, Q1 was printed in 1600 by James Roberts for Thomas Heyes. The manuscript text of *Merchant of Venice* was registered on July 22, 1598 to James Roberts. The wording of the registration is peculiar:

1598, 27 July, James Robertes. Entered for his copy under the hands of both the wardens, a booke of the Marchaunt of Venyce, or otherwise called the Jewe of Venyce. Provided that it be not printed by the said James Robertes or any other whatsoever without license first had from the Right Honorable the Lord Chamberlain. Sixpence paid

It is not known what happened to prevent Roberts from obtaining immediate license from the Lord Chamberlain, but *Merchant* sat in manuscript form for two more years. On October 28, 1600, a new entry in the Stationers' log indicates that the copyright of *Merchant* was transferred to Hayes. This allows us to date the printing of the *Merchant* Q1 to October 1600.

On the title page of the quarto, credit is given to the William Shakespeare brand-name, but this attribution is softened somewhat by the block print emblem between the lines. This is not the familiar V-Block associated with de Vere, and at present, I am unable to trace the motif, which was a standard decorative block. But that is not the same as saying that it doesn't mean anything. There is, however, one suggestive "clue" in the title page blurb:

**As it hath beene divers** times acted by the Lord Chamberlaine his Servants.
(As it hath beene **Di Ver's**)

### The Merry Wives of Windsor, Q1

*The Merry Wives of Windsor*, Q1 was printed in 1602 by Thomas Creede for Arthur Johnson. This is classified as a bad text quarto, but that is by comparison with the *Folio*, 1623 version.

Several elements of the title-page design are suggestive of a covert nod towards the Earl of Oxford's authorship. Notice that the V-Block print favored by de Vere has been used to form an ornamental device. Creede had used this V-Block before, directly conjunct de Vere's name, as we have seen before.

The blurb that names the provenance of the play echoes the *Merchant* quarto in saying:

As it hath been divers

The layout also produces an interesting word alignment.

**By** William Shakespeare

As it hath bene **diver**s times Acted by the right Honorable
my Lord **Chamberlaine**s servants. Both before her
**Majestie**, and else - where.

Reading straight down from the word "By" we can see: **By /di ver / Chamberlaine / Majestie.** *Majesty*, as a word, refers to the "Greatness" of a sovereign. *Majesty* is related to *Major* and shares the same deep root "*mag*" with *Magnus*, great. So, by my interpretation, the word game here implies: **By de Vere, Great Chamberlain.**

A

# Moſt pleaſaunt and

excellent conceited Co-
medie, of Syr *Iohn Falſtaffe*, and the
merrie Wiues of *Windſor*.

## Entermixed with ſundrie

variable and pleaſing humors, of Syr *Hugh*
the Welch Knight, Iuſtice *Shallow* , and his
wiſe Couſin M. *Slender*.

With the ſwaggering vaine of Auncient
*Piſtoll*, and Corporall *Nym*.

By *William Shakeſpeare*.

As it hath bene diuers times Acted by the right Honorable
my Lord Chamberlaines ſeruants. Both before her
Maieſtie, and elſe-where.

**LONDON**
Printed by T. C. for Arthur Iohnſon, and are to be ſold at
his ſhop in Powles Church yard, at the ſigne of the
Flower de Leuſe and the Crowne.
**1602.**

*Merry Wives of Windsor*, Q1 title page.

## Hamlet

*Hamlet* first appeared in Quarto in 1603. This Q1 is generally considered a "bad" quarto because it does not contain the full text as in the Q2 of 1604. Also, much of the famous dialogue is significantly different from what we are used to in the standard text. One theory, not widely accepted, is that the 1603 *Hamlet* is based on a surviving text of the lost "ur-Hamlet", an early version of the drama that was remarked upon in the 1580's. Perhaps the appearance of the old play prompted the author to rewrite the play, and, a year later, to "release" the complete and updated play to the publisher, Ling. The orthodox theory of *Hamlet* is that the first quarto, 1603, was simply a bungled attempt to produce a text of the play, for commercial reasons, without an authentic manuscript copy.

The actual printer of *Hamlet*, Q1 is not named, but the publishers were Nicholas Ling and John Trundell. Bibliographic scholarship suggests that Valentine Simmes was the actual printer, with Roberts' press running off a few of the pages.

For whatever reason, this title page contains some of the cleverest clues, "hiding in plain sight", that we have yet seen. The "credit" is given as:   By William Shake-speare.   Note the hyphen in "Shake - speare." and the period that follows it. Note that unlike the other title pages, that have frequent periods in the text and titles, the period at the end of "Shake - speare." is the *only* period used above the Emblem. Periods are used to shorten words and phrases by abbreviation. They inform the reader that something has been left out. The combined use of hyphen and period are just one more indication that this *William  Shake - speare* is a pseudonym.

Now look at the bizarre typeset layout of the descriptive paragraph :

As it hath beene diverse times  acted **by his Highnesse ser -** vants in the Cittie of London  :   **as also** in the two **V -** niversities of  Cambridge and **Oxford**, and  else-wh**e re**

Why did the printer split the words "servants" and "Universities"? The empty space on the left hand side cries out for the letters "ser" and "V". To my eye, the reason for the strange typesetting is clear; by reading just the rightmost characters on these three lines we get :

**ser -**
**V -**
**ere**

As in : "Sir V ere"

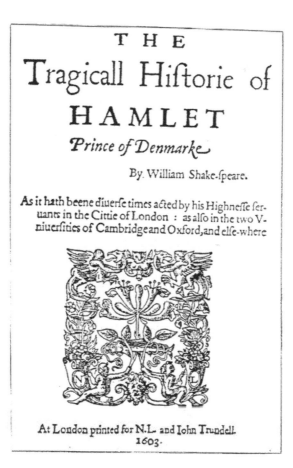

*Hamlet*, Q1 title page.

Using " Ser Vere " as a starting point , one can also read :

**by his Highnesse ser-**
**as also          V-**
**Oxford          ere**

(by his highness Sir Vere, as also Oxford)

Now it must be noted that no one would actually refer to the Earl of Oxford as "Sir", in conversational address. He was not known to have been knighted, and calling him *Sir* to his face would have been a social faux pas. The correct honorific for de Vere was *Lord* Oxford. But what we are discussing here are playful word games I believe are the result of the publishers having a little fun.

**Ling emblem,** enlarged from from title page of *Hamlet* Q1.

Now to the emblem. This cryptic figure is usually described as the emblem of Nicholas Ling, because of the N. L. letters and the fish, which is apparently a Ling fish. The emblem was used prior to 1603, so there it cannot have been designed for or intended for *Hamlet*.

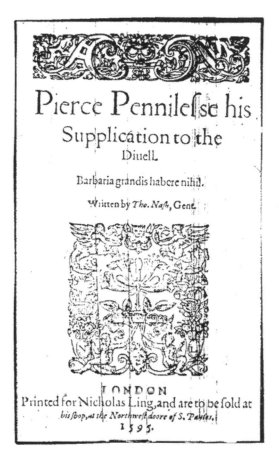

*Pierce Penniless*, Q5, title page.

McKerrow lists this as emblem #301. He cites the first use on a reprint of *Pierce Penilesse*, (the Q5 of 1595) by Thomas Nashe. *Pierce Penilesse* was first printed in 1592, and quickly ran through 3 editions; the Q4 was printed in 1593. With its sensational "I negotiated with Satan" theme, *PP* was one of the true "best sellers" of the 1590's. The significance of the Q5 of *Pierce Penilesse*, 1595, is that it was printed by Thomas Creede for Nicholas Ling. In other words, around 1595, Ling acquired the rights to *PP* from its previous publisher John Busby. As Ling was not a printer, he brought in Creede to reset and print the book. Coincident to this, Ling acquires a

177

brand new woodcut emblem and uses it on the new reprint of *Pierce Penilesse*. Ling goes on to publish many books, but he doesn't always use this emblem. It is used occasionally, and *Hamlet* is its most famous appearance, (on both the 1603 "bad" quarto and the 1604 "good" quarto). The Q5 of *Pierce Penilesse*, 1595, (Creede for Ling), was the final printing of the book, but the first use of the new emblem. And there is an Oxford connection to this book. In the opening Epistle, written in 1592 for the second edition, Nashe defends himself on various points, and apologizes that explanations couldn't be provided in the first edition, because he was not in London due to the plague. He writes:

> These were prepared for *Pierce Penilesse*' first setting foorth, had not the fear of infection detained me with my Lord in the Country.

Space does not permit an explanation, but there are reasons to believe that Oxford was the Lord who was patronizing Nashe in the exact time period specified in the Epistle, based on their known literary relationship, and the chronology of both men. To be fair, the orthodox biography of Nashe claims, with no more "proof" than I can offer in competition, that the patron here referred to by Nashe was Archbishop Whitgift.

Another interesting use of the rebus emblem is on the Q3 of the Ben Jonson play, *Every Man Out of His Humour*. This is the play that seems to have clear allusions to Shaksper-of-Stratford as the country fool Sogliardo. Other aspects of the plot seem to involve the Earl of Oxford. The play was printed in 1600 in three different Quartos, for two different publishers, and by apparently three different printers. It is not as simple as a sequential transfer of rights. It seems that London was flooded with the play, by farming the rights out to separate distribution channels. One of the three, Ling's, might be a pirate copy, but there is little evidence either way. According to the standard Jonson scholarship, the Q1 of *Every Man Out*, 1600 is the one that was printed *for* William Holme, and features an odd woodcut emblem of two winged devils attending a vase. The Q2 is assigned to the quarto printed for William Holme that uses the "Blazing Book" emblem (with P S) used by Peter Short. The Q3 of *Every Man Out* was printed, 1600, for Nicholas Ling and features the emblem that would later decorate *Hamlet*. E.K. Chambers says that the Ling version is the sloppiest print job of the three. I don't think that helps my theory, but I'd rather not suppress evidence. *Pierce Penilesse* and *Every Man Out* are two works that reveal much about the Oxford – "Shakespeare" puzzle, from contemporary writers who knew the Earl of Oxford.

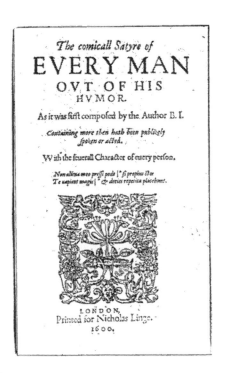

*Every Man Out of His Humor*, Q3, title page.

Having said all that, and being mindful that the emblem first appeared in 1595, the graphic symbolism of the emblem used on *Hamlet* has elements that do not belong simply to "a rebus on the name of Ling", which is the standard explanation. It appears to me that the device contains some of the same category of Vere symbols and puns we have been cataloging.

Look again at the emblem: At the bottom of the figure is the face of a Green Man. Flanking the Green Man are two cherubs or nymphs, each holding a quill pen, and a V shaped branch . The two V's form a W that holds a fish. The animal is a Ling fish, a skinny creature whose name derives from the Indo-European "lingam".

The fish is caught up "in the two V's", a phrase echoed on the *Hamlet* Q1 title page. But the fish also appears to be wrapped up in a string or fishing line. In Latin, the word for a fisherman's drag-line is:  Everriculum!

Above the fish is a peculiar flower with V shaped blooms. McKerrow, in his book of printer's emblems, says it is a Honeysuckle.

Shakespeare, in *Much Ado about Nothing* has Hero explain the mythic significance of the honeysuckle.

Hero:           …Say that thou overheard'st us
                And bid her steal into the pleached bower,
                **Where honeysuckles, ripened by the sun,**
                **Forbid the sun to enter; like favourites,**
                **Made proud by princes, that advance their pride**
                **Against that power that bred it. There will she hide** her,
                To listen our propose. This is thy office.
                Bear thee well in it and leave us alone.
                  *Much Ado*  Act III, Scene I.

The suggestion is that Honeysuckles represent  arrogant courage against ultimate authority. They offer a place to hide. The lead characters in *Pierce Penniless* and *Hamlet* both stand up against the highest levels of Authority. Lord Oxford, though influential socially, had little or no political power. By continuing to rail against those injustices he cared about, Oxford resisted the status-quo authority, and did so, in the 1590's through 1604 from behind a honeysuckle curtain.

 At the top of the emblem is an Owl. It is Athene / Minerva's Owl. The bird that says "Who?" "Who's there" is the opening line of *Hamlet.*

Notice also that the cherub on the lower left is touching his quill pen to the letter "N" in a cartouche. In his other hand, the letter "V". This cherub thus spells out "N. V." which is "Envy", a code word in several key "allusions to Shake-Speare". "To draw no envy (Shakespeare) on thy name..." says Ben Jonson in the *First Folio*. N. V. might stand for Ned Vere, Oxford's nickname, or for Nihil Verius, two thirds of his motto. Nihil Verius = "Nothing (so) True", or poetically, "Nothing (but) the Truth".

The cherub on the lower right does not mirror the action on the left. He does not point to the "L". On both sides of the emblem long snaky dragons with angels riding, rise up to threaten the Owl at the center. The Owl, however has turned the dragon's heads back to confront their riders. I'm still puzzling about what this might represent.

## *Hamlet*, Q2

*Hamlet*, Q2, was printed in 1604, by James Roberts for Nicholas Ling. This is the expanded, "Good" Quarto.

The emblem remains, but the paragraph that contained "Oxford " and "Ser Vere" has been replaced with a new blurb. Perhaps the clues on the 1603 page were considered too blatant. One new hint remains in the new blurb:

according to the **true** .

# *THE*
# Tragicall Historie of
# HAMLET,

*Prince of Denmarke.*

By William Shakespeare.

Newly imprinted and enlarged to almoſt as much
againe as it was, according to the true and perfect
Coppie.

**AT LONDON,**
Printed by I. R. for N. L. and are to be ſold at his
ſhoppe vnder Saint Dunſtons Church in
Fleetſtreet. 1604.

*Hamlet,* **Q2,** title page.

# Chapter Twelve

# The Quartos 1605 - 1622

The publications of Shakespeare plays that appeared after Oxford's Death in 1604 are:

*King Lear*, Q1, 1608 printed by Nathaniel Butler.
*Troilus and Cressida*, Q1, 1609, printed by G. Eld.
*Pericles*, Q1, 1609, from an unknown printer.
*Othello*, Q1, 1622 printed by Nicholas Okes.

New Shakespeare plays (mostly anonymous) had appeared in print steadily from 1594 to 1603 and then the output dropped off severely. The standard argument used by anti-Oxfordians is that Edward de Vere's death in 1604 rules him out as the author of works that were published afterwards. But this rebuttal is hollow. The vast majority of professional writers, past and present, leave unpublished works at their deaths. The steady stream of "Shakespeare-related" publications literally stopped dead after the 1604 *Hamlet*. Then, from 1608 to 1622, which includes the era when Shaksper-of-Stratford is imagined to have been at the peak of productivity and talent, only the *Sonnets*, and four more canon plays appeared. But the *Sonnets* existed long before 1609. Meres mentioned them in 1598, in *Palladis Tamia*. And the plays *Lear*, *Troilus*, *Pericles*, and *Othello* are all arguably older court and repertory plays from Oxford's companies.

## *King Lear*, Q1

*King Lear*, Q1 was printed by N. Okes for Nathaniel Butter in 1608. Nathaniel Butter was a publisher, and later a journalist. His career began when he was admitted as a freeman of the Stationers' Company in 1604. Four years later he was able to set up his own bookshop, the Pide Bull. A "pied" or "piebald" bull, is another reminder of Apis the Bull, a favorite symbol of Oxford. Pied means splotchy or multi-colored. Recall the Pied Piper.

## M. William Shak-speare:

### *HIS*
True Chronicle Historie of the life and
death of King L E A R and his three
Daughters.

*With the vnfortunate life of* Edgar, *sonne*
and heire to the Earle of Gloster, and his
sullen and assumed humor of
T o m of Bedlam :

*As it was played before the Kings Maiestie at Whitehall vpon*
*5. Stephans night in Christmas Hollidayes.*

By his Maiesties seruants playing vsually at the Gloabe
on the Bancke-side.

*LONDON,*
Printed for *Nathaniel Butter*, and are to be fold at his shop in *Pauls*
Church-yard at the signe of the Pide Bull neere
St. *Austins* Gate. 1 6 0 8.

*King Lear*, Q1, title page.

*King Lear* was one of the first publications by Butter after establishing the Pide Bull. According to McKerrow, the emblem used here by Butter had passed through several owners and is of unclear origin. But McKerrow states that this Pegasus emblem, #316, was used for the first time by

Butter on *King Lear*, 1608. He describes it "the device of a Pegasus above a caduceus and cornucopia upheld by hands emerging from clouds."

This edition of *King Lear* is considered a "bad" quarto, but not for the usual reasons. The text of *King Lear* Q1 is longer, not shorter, than the *Folio* version. There are twelve copies of the quarto known in existence today, and there are ten different *states* of the text therein, because the book was proofread and corrected during the printing process, and each book contains more, or less, of the corrections, depending on which pile of pages each book was collated out of. Paper was too valuable to just waste pages with errors. Those pages were used, and thus each copy of the finished book had slight variations.

There are no obvious typeset or emblematic clues on this title page, but the hyphen in "Shak-speare", a spelling never used by the Stratford man, continues the suggestion of brand-name merchandise.

*Lear* as a play however is extremely suggestive of the life and concerns of Oxford, who like Lear, divided his legacy among three daughters.

### *Troilus and Cressida*, Q1

*The History of Troylus and Cresseida* appeared in 1609. The printer was George Eld. This a "Good" Quarto. What appear to be two different quartos of 1609, are actually the same publication with two different title pages. Version 1 has a title-page blurb that says the play was recently acted by "the Kings majesties servants at the Globe."

## THE
# Hiftorie of Troylus
### and Crefleida.

*As it was afted by the Kings Maiefties*
feruants at the Globe.

*Written by* William Shakefpeare.

## THE
# Famous Hiftorie of
### Troylus *and* Crefleid.

*Excellently expreffing the beginning*
of their loues, with the conceited wooing
of *Pandarus* Prince of *Lisia*.

*Written by* William Shakefpeare.

LONDON
Imprinted by *G.Eld* for *R. Bonian* and *H. Walley*, and
are to be folde at the fpred Eagle in Paules
Church-yeard, ouer againft the
great North doore.
1609.

LONDON
Imprinted by *G.Eld* for *R. Bonian* and *H. Walley*, and
are to be fold at the fpred Eagle in Paules
Church-yeard, ouer againft the
great North doore.
1609.

*Troilus and Cressida*, Q1, alternate title pages.

Version 2 removes the above claim, and adds a descriptive blurb. Inside there is a two page introduction or "Epistle". This fascinating piece of prose states that the drama within is a new play, "... never staled with the Stage, never clapper-clawed with the palmes of the vulger...", a statement in direct contradiction to the claim on Version 1, that the play had been acted by the King's Men. I reproduce here the entire Epistle:

# A never writer, to an ever reader. Newes.

**Eternall reader, you have here a new play, never staled with the stage, never clapper-clawed with the palms of the vulgar**, and yet passing full of the palm **comical**; for it is a birth of your brain that never undertook anything comical vainly. **And were but the vain names of comedies changed for titles of commodities, or of plays for pleas, you should see all those grand censors, that now study them such vanities, flock to them for the main grace of their gravities, especially this author's comedies, that are so framed to**

186

the life that they serve for the most common commentaries of all the actions of our lives, showing such a dexterity and power of wit that the most displeased with plays are pleased with his comedies. And all such dull and heavy-witted worldings as were never capable of the wit of a comedy, coming by report of them to his representations, have found that wit there that they never found in themselves and have parted better witted than they came, feeling an edge of wit set upon them more than ever they dreamed they had brain to grind it on. So much and such savored salt of wit is in his comedies that they seem, for their height of pleasure, to be born in that sea that brought forth Venus. Amongst all there is none more witty than this: and had I time I would comment upon it, though I know it needs not, for so much as will make you think your testern well bestowed, but for so much worth as even poor I know to be stuffed in it. It deserves such a labor as well as the best comedy in Terrence or Plautus. **And believe this, that when he is gone and his comedies out of sale, you will scramble for them and set up a new English Inquisition.** Take this for a warning, and at the peril of your pleasure's loss, and judgments's, refuse not, nor like this the less for not being sullied with the smoky breath of the multitude; **but thank fortune for the 'scape it hath made amongst you, since by the grand possessers' wills I believe you should have prayed for them rather than been prayed.** And so I leave all such to be prayed for, for the state of their wits' healths, that will not praise it.  Vale.

*Troilus and Creseida* is classified as one of Shakespeare's Tragedies. Yet in this quarto, it is described on the cover as a History, and in the above introduction as a Comedy. True, it is all three, but there also seems to be a mismatch in the marketing concept of the quarto. In fact, there is no particular reason to believe that the above epistle necessarily matches the play it has been affixed to. The author warns: "… believe this, that when he is gone and his comedies out of sale, you will scramble for them and set up a new English Inquisition." If the introduction was written in 1609, it might argue against Oxford's involvement. But the play *Troilus and Creseida* was entered in the Stationers' Register on February 7, 1603 by James Roberts:

Entered for his copie in Full Court holden this day to print when he hath gotten sufficient authority for it. The booke of Troilus and Cressida as it is acted by my Lord Chamberlains Men.

If the play text existed in 1603, there is no reason that the introduction couldn't date from that year, when de Vere had but a year to live, and probably knew it. The introduction is completely in his style, that is the style of Shakespeare.

Roberts never printed Troilus (or such a copy no longer exists) and he died around 1607. His copyrights were thereafter assigned, wholesale, to William Jaggard. It is not clear how Richard Bonian and Henry Walley obtained ownership of the play, but they registered Troilus anew, on January 28, 1609.

> Entered for their Copy under the hand of Mr. Segar deputy to Sr. George Bucke and Mr. Warden Lownes, a booke called, The history of Troylus and Cressida.

In the epistle, the author warns that the "grand possessors" of the plays can not be expected to let any more plays escape their clutches. "Grand possessors" sounds a bit more political than just the controlling executives of acting companies.

The epistle to the reader begins:

> A never writer, to an ever reader.  Newes.

A nE.Ver writer to an E.Ver reader. Does this need explanation?

### *Pericles*, Q1

*Pericles, Prince of Tyre*, Q1, 1609 was printed by William White for Henry Gosson. The play itself is controversial in terms of authorship, even within the paradigm of Stratfordian certainty. "Shakespeare" had grown to despise long winded play titles, and the ridiculous weight and pretension of the full title of *Pericles*, as published in 1609, leads standard scholars to state that the author was completely out of the loop when this play found its way to print. The full title reads:

> *The late and much admired Play, called Pericles, Prince of Tyre. With the true Relation of the whole Historie, adventures, and fortunes of the said*

*Prince: As also The no less strange, and worthy accidents, in the Birth and Life, of his Daughter Mariana.*

THE LATE,

And much admired Play,
Called

Pericles, Prince
of Tyre.

With the true Relation of the whole Hiſtorie,
aduentures,and fortunes of the ſaid Prince:
As alſo,
The no leſſe ſtrange,and worthy accidents,
in the Birth and Life,of his Daughter
*MARIANA.*

As it hath been diuers and ſundry times acted by
his Maieſties Seruants,at the Globe on
the Banck-ſide.

By William Shakeſpeare.

Imprinted at London for *Henry Goſſon*,and are
to be ſold at the ſigne of the Sunne in
Pater-noſter row, &c.
1 6 0 9.

*Pericles, Prince of Tyre*, Q1, title page.

The play had been registered on May, 20, 1608 by Edward Blount. It is not known why Blount did not publish *Pericles*, or how White and Gosson got involved in the project.

There is an interesting connection between de Vere and the play. Standard scholars have concluded that one of the principal sources that "Shakespeare" drew on to write *Pericles*, was the 1576 book by Lawrence Twine called:

189

*The Patterne of Painefull Adventures, containing the most excellent, pleasant, and variable Historie of strange Accidents that befell unto Prince Apollonius, the Lady Lucina his wife, and Tharsia his daughter. Wherein the Uncertainty of this world and fickle state of man's life are lively described. Gathered into English by Laurence Twine Gentleman.*

*Patterne of Painefull Adventures* Q1 was printed in 1576, the Q2 in 1595 by V. Simmes, and the Q3 in 1607. The standard story is that "Shakespeare" was inspired by the 1607 edition, and turned the story into a play. But the topical allusions in the play that Shakespeare introduced relate more to the 1570's than to 1607.

Moreover, the Earl of Oxford actually knew Lawrence Twine, and was friends with Lawrence and his brother Thomas.

Thomas Twine M.D. (1543-1613) and his older brother Lawrence Twine, were extremely well educated and part of the movement in Elizabethan England, to translate classical works of every variety from Greek and Latin, into English, for publication.

Thomas Twine's first book, *The Breviary of Britain*, 1573, was a translation of a geographical history of England, originally in Latin by one Humfrey Lluyd. *Breviary of Britain* features a dedication to the Earl of Oxford, and, as it was well printed by Richard Jones in 1573, it can be argued that Oxford paid for the publication. Lawrence Twine contributed some verses to the *Breviary of Britain*. The Twine brothers unquestionably fell under de Vere's patronage around 1573. Three years later Lawrence released his translation of *The Patterne of Painefull Adventures*, which became one of the prime sources for *Pericles*. Standard scholars are puzzled because they perceive that  Shakespeare's *Pericles* is an example of his talent being off. They believe *Pericles* was written after *Hamlet*, and the quality is just so much lower, that the only conclusion to draw is that Shakespeare didn't really write the play, or that others embellished an abandoned project and capitalized on Shakespeare's name. But if we postulate that *Pericles* was written by Oxford in the late 1570's, it would have been one of the first "Shakespeare" plays, not one of the last. As a youthful play, it becomes magnificent; even the long winded title, which the "17th century Shakespeare" despised, would have been acceptable and amusing, in the heady Euphuistic days of the 1570's.

*Pericles* features a Tournament in which the hero wins a bride. Oxford was competing and winning Royal Tournaments in this era. Shaksper-of-Stratford never jousted. That's for certain.

*Pericles* was the one play left out of the *First Folio*, and even the *Second Folio*, 1632. *Pericles* became semi-acceptable as a Shakespeare play with its registration and inclusion into the 3rd *Folio* of Shakespeare, 1664.

## Othello, Q1

*Othello*, Q1 was printed in 1622 by Nicholas Okes for Thomas Walkley. *Othello* was registered on October 6, 1621 to Thomas Walkley. *Othello* Q1, printed by Okes, followed in 1622. *Othello* is one of Shakespeare's classic Tragedies. It was never printed during the lifetime of Oxford, but neither was it printed in the lifetime of Shaksper, who died in 1616. So when was *Othello* written? The allusions point to the 1580's. But we know it was written before 1604, because *Othello* was recorded as having been played before King James at Whitehall on November 1st, 1604. Oxford is reported to have died on June 24, 1604. His daughter Susan de Vere married Philip Herbert, the Earl of Montgomery in an elaborate royal style wedding at Whitehall over Christmas of 1604. During the Christmas season of 1604-1605, King James was entertained with no less than seven private productions of Shakespeare plays, some never seen (or recorded) before, like *Othello*. It is transparently obvious, within the Oxfordian paradigm, that Susan de Vere, the Countess Montgomery, had something to do with magnificent play scripts appearing (out of locked cabinets) just in time to entertain her new King.

*Othello*, Q1, title page.

Still, the text of *Othello* was still held tightly until 1621-22, when the manuscript was readied for commercial publication. Because *Othello* is so overtly political, it is not impossible that the publication in 1622 was partly for money, and partly an effort by the publisher (who may have been handed cash by someone, like Henry de Vere, the 18th Earl of Oxford) to send a message to society about secrets and lies, and the scheming that men do to grab power from others.

There are some enigmatic aspects to the *Othello* Q1 publication. The blurb states:

*As it hath beene d i v e r s e time s acted at the*
# Globe, and **at the Black-Friars**, by
*his Majesties Servants.*

Recall that Edward **de Vere** was one of the originators of producing plays at the **Black Friars** hall. Remember also that a prime source for *Othello* was *Hekatompathia*, which was first published in English by the efforts of the Earl of Oxford, who edited, and co-wrote the book with Thomas Watson. The book is dedicated to Oxford.

The emblem here is the Pegasus used by Nathaniel Butter on the Pied Bull quarto of King Lear. McKerrow didn't know how the woodcut passed to Walkley, but I do. Since McKerrow's day it has been learned that the same printer, Nicholas Okes, was responsible for *King Lear* 1608, and *Othello*, 1622. Okes' name doesn't appear on the Pied Bull *Lear*, and that was the source of the confusion.

On the inside of the Othello Q1 is a note from "The Stationer to the Reader." This paragraph strikes me as having some suggestive layout ciphers:

## The Stationer to the Reader.

To set forth a book without an Epistle, were like to the old English proverbe , A **blew coat without a badge**, & *the Au-thor being dead* , I thought good to take that piece of worke upon mee : To com-mend it, I will not, for that which is good , I hope every man will commend, without intreaty : and I am the bol-der , because the **Authors name** is sufficient to vent his worke. Thus leaving **every** one to the liberty of judge-ment : I have ventered to print this Play, and leave it to the generall censure.
Yours,

Thomas **V V** alkley

Oxford's servants wore Blue coats. To wear a "blue coat without a badge" is to be dressed incompletely. (Oxford's men wore a blue livery coat with a blue boar badge). The author is declared dead, which was true for Oxford as well as Shaksper in 1622, but it does put Francis Bacon out of the running. (Bacon died in 1626).

The typeset layout forces **Authors name** to stand directly above **every**. Probably just another coincidence.

This completes the analysis of the Shakespeare first edition quartos. After the *Folio* was printed in 1623, the public perception of Shakespeare the author and Shakespeare the man began to change. The authorship of this whole group of plays had been a quiet enigma, probably un-noticed, and irrelevant to the vast majority of Jacobean citizenry. The 1623 *Folio* cemented the myth of "Shakespeare", the imagined rustic genius of Stratford-on-Avon.

# Chapter Thirteen

# The Poetry Quartos

## *Venus & Adonis*, Q1

In contrast to the early publication of the "Shakespeare" plays, which were mostly anonymous, the poetry ascribed to Shakespeare was always printed with the cover name. The first appearance of the name William Shakespeare, as the writer of a published work, was on an inside page of Venus & Adonis Q1, 1593. The poem Venus & Adonis concerns the flawed seduction of young Adonis by the Goddess Venus, and his tragic death, being gored to death by a **wild boar**.

Venus & Adonis was registered on April 18, 1593 to Richard Field, and probably was available for sale that day. Most publications were registered hot off the press. There was no incentive to spend the sixpence for registration until it became legally necessary. Richard Field hailed from Stratford-on-Avon, and thus the orthodox interpretation is that Shaksper knew Field from his hometown, and took his poem to someone he knew. But there are no links which put Shaksper and Field together. My hypothesis is that Oxford, who had already had material published by both Field, and the Venus & Adonis bookseller, John Harrison, was introduced to the name and existence of a person named "William Shaksper" through Field, and that this was the moment that Oxford hit upon the idea of using this man as a cover for a new round of publications. Oxford was already known as the Spear Shaker, so running into an opportunity to print racy or controversial material under a cover name that had plausible deniability, through the front of Mr. "Shaksper" was probably appealing.

# VENVS
# AND ADONIS

*Vilia miretur vulgus : mihi flauus Apollo*
*Pocula Caſtalia plena miniſtret aqua.*

LONDON

Imprinted by Richard Field, and are to be ſold at
the ſigne of the white Greyhound in
Paules Church-yard.
1593.

Richard Field, 1561 - 1624, came to London sometime before 1579 when he began his apprenticeship with publisher George Bishop. During his apprenticeship, Bishop published a book for the Earl of Oxford: Diverse Sermons of Calvin by Thomas Stocker, 1581. This book has an extremely long dedication to Edward de Vere, with Stocker thanking him for his patronage. Oxford had been in trouble due to his affair with Anne Vavasour, and was attempting to get back in the good graces of his wife Anne Cecil, the Countess Oxford, by expressing repentance and religious transformation. Several publications were sponsored by Oxford in an apparent attempt to convince his estranged wife of his fealty. The strategy appears to have worked, as the two got back together and had more children. Richard Field was transferred, the mid 1580's to the shop of the famous printer Vautrollier, and Field made the bold business move of marrying Vautrolier's widow in 1587, acquiring Vautrolier's shop, presses, and copyrights with one "I do". Field took over the use of Vautrolier's famous emblem, which shows "the Anchor of Hope", "Anchora Spei".

This is the emblem that decorates the title page of Venus & Adonis. There are more links between Oxford and Field. The important book: The Arte of English Poesy, was first printed in 1589 by Richard Field. The book had been registered on Nov.9, 1588 to Thomas Orwin, but was re-assigned to Field on April 7, 1589. The Arte of English Poesy describes Oxford as a brilliant poet, and features an Oxford Poem. In 1596, Field printed Spenser's Faerie Queene, enlarged. Faerie Queene contains 14 dedication poems by Spenser to the nobility of England. The 4th is addressed to Oxford. Spenser's praise begins:

> Receive, most noble Lord in gentle gree,
> The unripe fruit of an unready wit:
> Which by thy **countenance** doth crave to be
> Defended from foul **Envy's** poisonous bit.

Spenser's use of the word countenance recalls Harvey's epithet for Oxford: Vultus Tela Vibrat. "Thy countenance shakes a spear" or "Thy will shakes spears".

To draw no envy (Shakespeare) on thy name..." is the first line of Jonson's poem to Shakespeare in the *First Folio*. He says he does not want to associate *Envy* with the name

*Shakespeare*. Recall that N.V. is Nihil Verius, Nothing but the Truth, and N.V. was also Ned Vere, almost certainly what his close friends knew him as. In the Shakespeare plays, characters named Edward are frequently referred to as "Ned".

Field continued to print Oxford-related material in the decade that followed *Venus & Adonis*, 1593.
*Ecclesiastes*, by Henry Lok, 1597 was printed by Richard Field. It has multiple dedications, including a prominent address to the Earl of Oxford. It was Field, who printed for George Bishop in 1603, a new edition (Q5) of the Oxford-sponsored *The Courtier* in Latin.

On the inside of *Venus & Adonis* is the famous dedication to Henry, the Earl of Southampton, signed William Shakespeare. Once again, extremely peculiar spelling, typeset, and line lengths have created a potential word game.

## TO THE RIGHT HONORABLE
### Henrie **V** Vriothesley, Earle of Southampton, and Baron of Titchfield.

R Ight Honourable , I know not how I shall offend in
dedicating my unpolisht lines to your Lordship, nor
how the worlde v v i l l censure **mee** for choosing so
strong a proppe to support so **v v**eake a burthen,
onelye if your Honour seeme but pleased , I ac-
count my selfe highly praised , and vowe to take advantage of all
idle houres, till I have honoured you **v v** i t h some graver labour. But
if the **first heire of my invention** prove deformed, I shall be sorie it
had **so noble a god-father** : **and never** after care so barren a land,
for feare it yeeld me still so bad a harvest , I leave it to your Honourable survey, and **your Honour** to **your** heart's content , vvhich I wish
may al vv ais ans vv **e r e** your o **vv** n e v v i s h and the v v orl ds hope -
ful expectation.

Your honour's in all duty,
William Shakespeare

The capital letters **E V** are seen vertically, by the use of "V V" in place of a "W" in Wriothesley. This suggests Edward **Vere**. Note that in the first line: "I know not how", and the third line, "how the worlde vvill censure mee...", the printer possessed and used a lowercase true "w" in the words "know", "how" and "worlde". A "w" is used in line six in the word "vowe", and at the end of line 11 in "wish". But every other potential "w" is replaced by "v v". This creates some interesting vertical word associations.

In Lines 3 and 4 are juxtaposed: **me / v v**.
In Line 7, 8, and 9 are aligned: **v v / prove / never**
Line 9: **so noble a god-father : and   never**
Lines 11 & 12 : **your Honour / v vere   your o v v ne   v v**

## The Rape of Lucrece

*The Rape of Lucrece*, Q1, 1594, was published by the same team of Field and Harrison. The header ornament used on the *Venus* and *Lucrece* quartos features a Goddess figure amidst vines, scroll work and two puck-like figures. Although it is tempting to identify the goddess as Venus, the two peacocks on either side of her suggest that this is Juno. The goddess Juno is mentioned throughout the Shakespeare plays, even putting in a personal appearance in the Tempest. Juno is associated, among other things, with marriage.

SONG:
> Wedding is great Juno's crown;
> O blessed bond of board and bed!
> 'Tis Hymen peoples every town;
> High wedlock then be honoured.
> Honour, high honour, and renown,
> To Hymen, god of every town!
> *As You Like It* Act 5, Scene 4

# LVCRECE.

LONDON.

Printed by Richard Field, for Iohn Harrifon;and are
to be fold at the figne of the white Greyhound
in Paules Churh-yard.  1594.

*The Rape of Lucrece*, Q1, title page.

Both poems *Venus and Adonis* and *Lucrece*, bear dedications
to Southampton. In the early 1590's Lord Burghley was
trying to convince young Southampton to marry his grand-
daughter, Elizabeth Vere, Oxford's eldest daughter.
Southampton had to pay a hefty fine for refusing the

200

marriage. A plausible explanation of the two dedications to Southampton is that they are either remnants of Oxford's interest in Southampton as a potential son-in-law, or after-the-fact remembrances of what might have been. Both poems involve seduction. Both printed quartos of the poems are under the sign of Juno.

The published poetry of Edward de Vere includes a lyric *Vain Desire*, which connects the goddesses Venus, Juno, and Pallas Athene, the triumvirate of Goddesses that "Shake-speare" was obsessed with. This poem had first appeared in the 1576 poetry collection *Paradyse of Dainty Devises*, which has numerous poems signed by Oxford, several of which are in the same verse form *as Venus & Adoni*s. In 1576, the poem was called "Beyng in love he complaineth". The 1596 sixth quarto of Paradyse, has enough emendations to suggest that Oxford doctored his old book for republication. The poem in 1596 is re-named *Coelum Non Solum*.

> If care or skill could conquer vain desire,
> Or reason's reins my strong affection stay,
> Then should my sights to quiet breast retire
> And shun such signs as **secret thoughts** bewray;
> Uncomely love, which now **lurks in my breast**
> Should cease my grief, through wisdom's power oppressed.
>
> But who can leave to look on **Venus'** face
> Or yieldeth not to **Juno's high estate**?
> What wit so wise as gives not **Pallas** place?
> These virtues rare each god did yield amate
> Save her alone who yet on earth doth reign,
> Whose beauty's string no gods can well distrain.
>   E.O.   From *Paradyse of Dainty Devises*, 1576

This excellent iambic pentameter, and the vocabulary of Vere's poem is echoed in *Lucrece* itself.

> Nor shall he smile at thee in **secret thought**,
> Nor laugh with his companions at thy state:
> But thou shalt know thy interest was not bought
> Basely with gold, but stol'n from forth thy gate.
>   *Lucrece* 1065-9

Why should the worm intrude the maiden bud?

201

Or hateful cuckoos hatch in sparrows' nests?
 Or toads infect fair founts with venom mud?
Or tyrant folly **lurk in gentle breasts**?
Or kings be breakers of their own behests?
  *Lucrece* 848 ff

For that he colour'd with his **high estate**,
Hiding base sin in plaits of majesty;
That nothing in him seem'd inordinate,
Save something too much wonder of his eye,
  *Lucrece* 92 ff

The Dedication to *Rape Of Lucrece* is every bit as odd as the dedication in *Venus & Adonis*.

# TO THE RIGHT
## HONORABLE, HENRY
V V riothesley, Earl of Southampton,
and Baron of Tichfield.

T H E love I dedicate to your
Lordship is without end; wher -
of this Pamphlet  without be -
ginning, is but a superfluous
Moity.  The warrant I have of
your  Honourable  disposition,
not  the worth of my  vntutored
Lines  makes  it assured of acceptance.  **V V** hat I have
done   is  yours;  what  I have to do**e is yours** ,  being
part in all  I  have , devoted yours.  **V V e r e** my  worth
greater, my duety  would shew **great**er,   meane time,
as it is, it is bound to your **Lord**ship;  To whom I wish
long life still lengthened with all happinesse.

Your lordship's in all duety,
William Shakespeare.

The printer uses the same method of exchanging **V V** for a regular **W**, as he sees fit. There is a perfectly normal capital **W** in the name William, at the bottom.

The word puzzle is seen among lines 8 - 12:
V V / is yours, Vere / great / Lord

The printer has also managed to line up the "e" in "doe" directly over the first V in **V Vere,** creating

   **e**

**V Vere**


## The Sonnets

In 1609 the *Sonnets* were published for the first time. The Printer was George Eld and the publisher, or agent, was Thomas Thorpe. There are two variant editions of the *Sonnets*, evidenced by the title pages. One names William Aspley as the bookseller, the other belongs to John Wright. This Q1 is considered authoritative, if slightly flawed. There is no other source for comparison. Later versions merely mangle or re-arrange the 1609 edition.

To orthodox scholars, the *Sonnets* are an enigma. The voice of the author, melancholy, and longing for youth, does not match the known biography or chronology of Shaksper. Elaborate theories have been created to find a context or explanation for Shaksper of Stratford's apparent secret life or dark side. Of course the Oxford hypothesis is, itself, an elaborate theory. But it has the advantage of actually fitting the facts, and being in likelihood, true.

Now to the Quarto: The title of the work is given as: SHAKE - SPEARES SONNETS. The use of all capital letters, and the use of the hyphen seem to indicate that what we have here is a Brand-Name, not an authors name. On the lower portion of the page are two conspicuous horizontal lines, creating an empty space. Author Richard Kennedy pointed out long ago that the empty space "between the lines" is significant because that is where the author's name often appeared in Elizabethan era publications. We also have the statement: Never before Imprinted.

# SHAKE-SPEARES

# S O N N E T S.

Neuer before Imprinted.

AT LONDON
By *G. Eld* for *T. T.* and are
to be folde by *william Apley.*
*1 6 0 9.*

I have explained previously the puns in "Never" as relevant to our concern.

The abstract Headpiece on the *Sonnets* is not unique to this publication. This woodblock print, in variations, was used by several different printers. The design is typical of a subtle theme that was propagated by the paper and printers trades:

The flourishing all-pervading bounty of nature, and apparently, the Goddess. On this Headpiece, two cherubs and two dolphins attend a central Goddess emerging from a vase. There are vines and flowers. Because of the headdress, this may be Juno again. Notice that there are two hares, a left-facing rabbit above the **K** in SHAKE, and a right-facing rabbit over the **A** in SPEARS. There is a strange coincidence that on the last page of the *Sonnets,* the letters K A are printed in an eye catching large type face for no apparent reason. There is a simple "standard explanation" though: the last page of the Sonnets portion of the quarto is the first page of the quarto's folded signature "K". The large "A" is the continuity marker to the next page which begins "A Lovers Complaint". However, none of the other signature marks or continuity words are **emboldened** like the K A. If attention is being pointed to the Title Page rabbits, *perhaps* these "Hares" are meant to stand for "Heirs" and the "dolphins" are "dauphins".

If you put your finger over the "T" in SONNETS, the title of the piece becomes :
"SHAKE-SPEARES   SONNE S".

Oxford left at least two living sons of his acknowledged blood. They were Henry de Vere, the 18th Earl, Oxford's heir and successor, and Sir Edward Veer, Oxford's son by Anne Vavasour. Edward de Vere left behind two sons, (as well as three daughters, as did King Lear), so the symbolism I am suggesting on this title page from the *Sonnets* is not completely out of line with historical reality. Many will be tempted to see the whole "heir of Shakespeare" symbol as a pointer to Henry Wriothesley, Earl of Southampton, who is conjectured to be another illegitimate son of de Vere. In any case, Oxford was clearly dead in 1609 when the *Sonnets* were printed, so we have no way of knowing whether his original motivations for writing and keeping the poems were appropriately reflected by the surprising quarto publication of the *Sonnets* in 1609.

This publication connects Eld, Thorpe, Aspley, Wright, and "W.H." (the mysterious procurer). Discovering the motivations and connections of these men may shed light on whether the Sonnets really "escaped", or were published with nodding acceptance by Vere heirs.

The dedication says that the author was now "ever-living", i.e. deceased. William Shaksper of Stratford-on-Avon was alive and well in 1609 and there is no explanation for why he would permit the publication of these scandalous poems if he had actually written them. In all likelihood, Mr. Shaksper couldn't even *read* them !

The same Headpiece (with the hares) appeared a year earlier on *The Merry Devil of Edmonton*, 1608, yet another Apocryphal Shakespearean play. It also has the Green Man emblem.

The *Sonnets'* dedication has been exhaustively decoded by numerous Oxfordian writers. I will sum up the state of the art on the cryptic dedication, with my own insights added to ideas first published by British researcher, Dr. John Rollett.


TO . THE . ONLIE. BEGETTER . OF.
**THESE** . INSVING . **SONNETS**
Mr . W . H . **ALL**. HAPPINESSE.
AND. THAT. ETERNITIE.
PROMISED
**BY**.


OVR . **EVER - LIVING** . POET.
V V I S H E T H.


**THE** . WELL-WISHING .
ADVENTURER . IN .
SETTING.
**FORTH**.

There are six lines in the first "triangle stanza", two lines in the second, and four lines in the last. "EDWARD DE VERE" features: **six** letters, **two** letters, and **four** letters. Rollett's method was to count every word or letter, which is "stopped" by a period, as a single unit. Starting at the beginning, one counts forward to the 6<sup>th</sup> word, then forward 2 more words, and then skips ahead 4 words, then repeats. The sequence of words is bolded above. To begin, count forward 6 words to THESE to start the sequence. This is the phrase Rollett decoded with the cipher key:

**THESE. SONNETS. ALL. BY. EVER. THE. FORTH.**
  +6       +2        +4    +6   +2    +4    +6

The line **OVR . EVER - LIVING . POET. WISHETH** contains an incredible anagram. I discovered this in 1997.

O V R.  E V E R L I V I N G.  P O E T.  W I S H E T H. =

V E R O  N I H I L  V E R I V S.  P O E T.  G E T  W. H.

or on a lighter note:

**V E R O  N I H I L  V E R I V S  GOT  THE  PEW**

That it is possible at all to wrangle de Vere's Latin motto of 15 letters out of a sentence of only 24 letters, without fudging the spelling one iota, is nothing short of amazing.

Mr. WILLIAM

# SHAKESPEARES

COMEDIES,
HISTORIES, &
TRAGEDIES.

Published according to the True Originall Copies.

*LONDON*
Printed by Isaac Iaggard, and Ed. Blount. 1623.

# Chapter Fourteen

# The First Folio

In 1623, the *First Folio of Shakespeare* gathered the previous quarto dramas with 18 previously unpublished plays. This standard number, 18 is debatable, depending on your opinion *of Taming of A Shrew,* and other anonymous apocryphal early versions of the plays, not yet accepted by the orthodoxy. Shaksper-of-Stratford died in 1616, and didn't mention any literary properties in his otherwise meticulous will. So regardless of who the author was who used the name "Shakespeare", we have the situation of *a wealth of material* surviving its creator.

The *First Folio* thanks the sponsors of the publication, Pembroke and Montgomery. The Earl of Montgomery, Philip Herbert, was the husband of Susan de Vere, Oxford's daughter. The Earl of Pembroke, William Herbert, was Philip's brother. In other words, there is a strong likelihood that the owners of the unpublished "Shakespeare" plays, were none other than Oxford's heirs and kin.

The *First Folio* of 1623 was printed by a consortium of bookmen, organized by Isaac Jaggard, the son of William Jaggard. This Deluxe edition of thirty-six plays is one of the most famous and valuable books in the world. It is the work that made "Shake-Speare" famous, and cemented the pseudonym and cover story for all time.

Hundreds, if not thousands of books have been written analyzing and finding hidden messages in the *Folio.* Not only the title page, but the introductory poems and dedications, and the text itself have all been mined for secrets. The feverish Baconians of the 1800's added up the numerical value of every single word in the *Folio.* I am in no position to pass judgment on such a wide range of theories. The Oxfordian arguments concerning the meaning and import of the introductory poems and dedications have been well argued by the Ogburn's books, Ruth Lloyd Miller's, and others. So much has been written already about these topics, and about interpreting the Droeshout engraving that I will be mum and stick to what I hope are a few new observations.

Look at the line directly above the illustration :

Published **according to the True** Originall Copies.

Hiding within is :

**according to the True O**

There is also a propitious coincidence of letters directly above " the True O". I cannot claim that this reading of the letters indicates a designed intention by the printer or publisher. Nevertheless there it is.

C OM **E D I E S,**
HIST **O R I E S,** &
T R A **G E DIE S,**
Published according to **the True** Originall Copies

I suggest that this can be read as "E. Dies, O Rise, G' Edie" (G' Edie = "Good Edie" as in "G' day") By making a sort of "Viv-isection" we can somewhat eliminate the "G" and read :

**"E. Dies, O Rise, Edie the True. O."**

"Edie the True " = Edward de Vere. O = Oxford.

On the next page of the *First Folio* is the dedication to the Earls of Pembroke and Montgomery. Above the text is a graphic emblem that has a strong suggestive link to Edward de Vere. The woodcut appears again, a few pages later on the table of contents page. (A Catalogue ...)

# A CATALOGVE

of the feuerall Comedies, Hiftories, and Tragedies contained in this Volume.

The *Folio* woodcut features twin birds, perhaps peacocks or vultures, twin archers, Twin rabbits (in the upper left and right corners facing out, two creatures that appear to be calgreyhounds in the lower right and left corners, and a strange "Indian Boy" in the center. It is an extremely peculiar piece, even in a oeuvre that is laced with peculiarity. The boy is depicted sitting cross legged. Although he wears a headdress of flowers, his bare chest and (twin phalli ?) suggest this is not Juno, but some sort of pixie or pookah.

Incredibly, this emblem on the *First Folio* of Shakespeare, is modeled on an emblem that first appeared on an Oxford related publication: *Hekatompathia*, of 1582. This book has already been discussed in Chapter 11.

The emblem on *Hekatompathia* is nearly identical to the *Folio* woodcut, except that the image on *Hekatompathia* ends abruptly on three sides, cutting out the rabbits completely and with only the heads of the calgreyhounds showing. But if you compare the two cuts closely, you will see that they are not the same exact design, and the later emblem completes what is missing in the original.

The calgreyhound is a mythical animal, that is found in British Heraldry in one place only. The Calgreyhound was used in the arms of the 13th - 16th Earls of Oxford. For some reason Edward de Vere ceased using the calgreyhounds personally, but their appearance in the emblems of

211

Hekatompathia, (which is dedicated to Oxford and contains brilliant editorial passages by him)
and in the *First Folio* strongly suggests an intentional symbolic reference. The presence of the Calgreyhounds was recently noted as well by British researcher Christopher Bird.

The last of the *Folio* preliminary pages also seems to contain a clever word-game or cipher, which I discovered in 1997. The text at the top of the page reads:

# The Workes of William Shakespeare

containing **all his** Comedies, Histories, and
Tragedies: **T r u e l y** set forth, according to their first
O R I G I N A L L

In the third line "Truely" is placed directly above the O in Originall.

One can read: **True**      and      e
O                O
Reading from the top one can make out:
 The Workes / all his / Truly / O

Or, in a poetic variation that requires no ciphering, just read the first 4 syllables of each of the 4 lines:

The Workes of Will
containing all
Tragedies True
Originall

# Part Three :

# Wounded Truth is Renewed

# Chapter Fifteen

# The Thomas Creede Connection

**Thomas Creede,** (c.1558 - 1616) was one of the best of the Elizabethan printers. He apprenticed with Thomas East, beginning his indenture-training October 7th, 1578. East had a long career as a London printer, his name appearing on books from 1576 to 1608. In the 1580's and 90's East was a prominent music publisher, printing works by William Byrd, Thomas Watson, and Thomas Morley. These three men all are linked to Oxford and incorporated some of his lyrics and poems into their own works.

Thomas East printed no less than 14 books linked to Oxford or his wife Countess Anne over a period of twenty years.

| Work | Year | Printer, Publisher | Relevance |
|---|---|---|---|
| *Psalms of David* tr. by A. Golding | 1571 | East & Middleton for Harrison & Byshop | ded. to Oxford |
| *A Christian Discourse* ..by J. Brooke | 1578 | East | ded. to Anne |
| *Epistle of Blessed Apostle St. Paul* (tr. by "Fleming") | 1580 | East | ded. to Anne |
| *Phioravanti's discourse on Surgery,* by John Hester | 1580 | East | ded. to Oxford, displays Vere Arms |
| *Euphues and his England,* Q1, by John Lyly | 1580 | East for G. Cawood | ded. to Oxford |
| *Epistle of St. Paul ...of Niels Hemmingsen* | 1581 | | ded. to Anne |
| *Euphues* Q2 | 1581 | East for G. Cawood | ded. to Oxford |
| *Euphues* Q3 | 1582 | East for G. Cawood | ded. to Oxford |
| *Gwydonius, Carde of Fancie* Q1, by R. Greene | 1584 | East for Ponsonby | ded. to Oxford |
| *Euphues* Q4 | 1584 | East for G. Cawood | ded. to Oxford |
| *Euphues* Q5 | 1586 | East for G. Cawood | ded. to Oxford |

| | | | |
|---|---|---|---|
| *Psalmes Sonets & Songs of sadness & piety,* by W. Byrd | 1588 | East the assignee of W.Byrd | contains an Oxford Poem set to music for 5 voices |
| *Euphues* Q6 | 1588 | | ded. to Oxford |
| *Plainsong (Diverse and sundry ways )* by John Farmer | 1591 | East for W. Byrd | ded. to Oxford |

It would be very hard to argue that Thomas East never came to the attention of the Earl of Oxford.

An apprenticeship would normally last only 7 years, which means that Creede probably became a full printer around 1585. Creede's name does not appear on books however, until 1593. Nevertheless, he was in the employ of East all those years and cut his teeth on such books as *Gwydonius, Carde of Fancie,* which also became the first book that Creede printed under his own name, as a revival publication in 1593.

The "Wounded Truth" emblem, Viressit Vulnere Veritas, is listed as #299 in McKerrow's book of emblems. He cites a 1st use by Creede in 1594 with *The Mirror of Popish Subtleties* by R. Abbot. But Creede printed 9 known books in 1594, and the Abbot is not necessarily the first. Before I list those books, we must back up a bit in Creede's career.

Thomas Creede graduated to his own print shop in 1593. In that year he registered a ballad and printed two books. Neither book has the Creede "Truth" emblem, so both McKerrow and I agree that the emblem had not been cut yet. What is significant is that Creede's first paid job, as an independent contractor, was the printing of two Robert Greene reprints: *Mamillia,* and *Gwydonius, The Card of Fancie.* The second book bears a lavish dedication to Edward de Vere. Greene had "died" to the public the year before, in 1592, and with *Groatsworth of Wit* and related books still fresh in the reading public's mind, someone chose to re-issue these decade old satires. As one of the two books printed by

Creede in 1593 is prominently dedicated to Oxford, and both texts seem to refer to the Vere social world, it is not impossible that Oxford paid or persuaded Ponsonby or Creede to have the books re-set. The two books are *Gwydonius Card of Fancie,* and *Mamillia.*

### Gwydonius. The Card of Fancie. Wherein the follie of the Carpet Knights is deciphered ...

By Robert Greene ... /    Printed by Th. C. for William Ponsonby 1593

To the Right Honorable, Edward de Vere Earle of Oxenford, Viscount Bulbecke ...

Mamillia. The second part of the triumph of Pallas  by Robert Greene, 1593.

The text  of *Gwydonius. The Card of Fancie,* 1593, follows the original, which was printed in 1584 by Creede's master Thomas East. The publisher is the same, William Ponsonby. *Card of Fancie* was reprinted in 1587 by James Roberts for Ponsonby, and then in 1593 by Creede. The text is virtually the same but the type-setting and line lengths are different. All three printers who worked on this book: East, Roberts, and Creede, are associated with other projects linked to Oxford.

The quarto was printed by Creede for Ponsonby. This work was originally entered in the Stationers' Register on Sep. 6, 1583, but no copy of a 1583 quarto of *Mamillia* is known to still exist. The 1593 Creede version is thus the earliest extant copy.

The dedication of Mamillia begins :

To the Right Worshipful, and his especiall friends, Robert Lee and Roger Portington Esquires ...

The principal dedicatee is curiously un-named. In standard studies of Robert Greene, the men Lee and Portington are *assumed* to be Cambridge buddies of Greene circa 1583. But Roger Portington would seem to be the architect who built

Italian style villas for some of the wealthiest of Elizabethan Aristocrats, and was certainly known to the Earl of Oxford.

*The First part of Mamilla : A Mirrour or Looking-glasse for the Ladies of England* dates back to a Stationers' Entry in Oct., 1580, and the earliest edition is from 1583. It is considered by Greene scholars to be Greene's first work. Both of the *Mamilla* books are allusive to the Earl of Oxford and his social world, but explaining that here would involve a huge digression.

Creede enters the world of publishing as a freeman of the Stationers' Company in 1593. His first paid job was to reprint two Robert Greene books, one dedicated to Oxford. In 1594, Creede emerged as a "major" printer; he acquired the Wounded Truth emblem and began to use it. The Creede publishing venture continued in earnest through 1617.

Creede's many books include important quartos that intersect with the Oxford-Shakespeare world. In the arrangement that follows of the 9 known Creede quartos from 1594, I list first chronologically, the quartos that were entered in the Stationers' Register, followed by those with no SR entry.

*The First part of the Contention* (the primitive *Henry the 6th, Part 2* ) 1594. Anonymous. SR: March 12, 1594 (This is either one of the earliest "Bad Shakespeare Quartos", or a decent script of an early touring version of the play)

*A Looking Glasse for London and England*, 1594, "Made by Thomas Lodge Gentleman, and Robert Greene." SR : May 14, 1594. (Loosely based on Greene's "Mamilla" as above, and almost certainly Oxford related)

*The True Tragedy of Richard III*, 1594. Anonymous. SR: June 19, 1954 (This is a hotly debated early Richard III play. Clear Oxford links have been argued by others.)

*The First part of the Tragicall raigne of Selimus, sometime Emperor of the Turkes* ... as was played by the Queens Majesties Players", 1594. Anonymous. (This play is often attributed to Greene, and is a near-Shakespeare-quality drama that some believe was written by de Vere.)

*Arisbas, Euphues amidst his slumbers* by "I. D.", 1594. This work is variously attributed to John Davison or John Dickenson. The book is a satellite or late cousin to the other Euphues books of the 1570's and 80's which were overtly Oxford related.)

*The Mirrour of Popish subtleties* by "R. Abbot", 1594. Propaganda with a flair, possible Oxford connection. The credited author is Robert Abbot, who was the Bishop of Salisbury

*The Troublesome and Hard adventures in Love* "translated" by "R.C.", 1594. Contains allusive references to "Diana".

*Epicedum, Funeral Songs for Helen Branch* by "W. Har", 1594.

*Epitaph... Helen Branch* by Philip Sidney, 1594.

So quite a few of the books printed by Creede in his debut season,1593-1594, are part and parcel of the Oxford-Shakespeare literary world. Oxford's name is mentioned several times, "Shaksper's" never. The Creede publishing venture continued in earnest through 1617, although the nature of new works published changed dramatically after 1604.

I present here a list of other Creede press quartos that intersect with the Oxford-Shakespeare world. They all feature the Wounded Truth Emblem :

*The Lamentable Tragedie of Locrine* by " VV. S." 1595 . This is an apocryphal "Shakespearean" play with claimed revisions by "VV.S."

*Colin Clouts Come home again* by "Ed. Spencer" (spelled wrong on purpose?), 1595. This is an odd and important book as it seems to reflect a real or imagined conversation between "Spenser", Raleigh, Oxford, and others. Oxford is thought to be the character "Cuddie".

*Menaechmi of Plautus*, translated by " VV. VV. " 1595. This is usually attributed to William Warner. *Menaechmi* is the primary "source" for Shakespeare's *Comedy of Errors*, and the publication followed a stage production of *Errors* at Grays Inn around Christmas of 1594.

*Greenes Groatsworth of Wit*, Q2, 1596 This was the first reprint of the infamous 1592 book, which contains the lines about "an upstart crow" and "Shake-scene" that are erroneously described by the orthodoxy as the first known criticism of Shakespeare the actor-playwright.

*The Shepherds Calendar*, 1597. A reprint of Spenser's 1579 work. The allusions to Vere are intact.

*The Mirror of Alchimy*, 1597. Indexed as a work of Roger Bacon, the 14th century Magus. This version also contains contemporary (1590's) material, that remains anonymous or un-attributed. I have a hunch that this book was another example of Oxford's contribution to the field of Alchemy, whether he actually wrote parts of it or merely commissioned it to be published. Interestingly, there is a discussion of the Mirror of Alchimy and the Creede emblem in a modern book by Charles Nicholl called "The Chemical Theater", 1980. Nicholl has also written about Marlowe and Nashe. Nicholl is apparently unaware of the broader history of the emblem, and conveniently unaware of the Shakespeare authorship problem, but this is what he writes concerning the emblem's meaning, inspired by its appearance on an Alchemy book :

> ... this virgo redimata represents Truth, as the surrounding legend makes clear. "Viressit vulnere veritas" means, literally, "truth grows green through injury". Truth, in other words, is refreshed and fortified by the trials it must undergo (as a plant "grows green" by being cut back). The device expresses this visually by the divine hand, issuing from a cloud to whip the princess: Truth with a scourge. This is, one suddenly sees, an image at the heart of King Lear. Cordelia is this Mercurial princess: she is actually described in the play as "truth whipped out" (*King Lear* 1/4/117) ...

Nicholl, Chemical Theater, pages 223-4

Nicholl has the metaphor right, but has taken liberty with his quote. The exact passage from Lear reads :

FOOL       Truth's a dog must to kennel, he must be whipt out, when Lady the brach may stand by the fire and stink.

A bit later in the same scene:

FOOL       I marvel what kin thou and thy daughters are: **they'll have me whipt for speaking true** ...

*Parismus, the Renowned Prince of Bohemia*, 1598. This is a long forgotten work, and seems like it emerged from the "School-of-Shakespeare." It is credited to "E. Forde", a non existent person, whose name seems to be yet another pseudonym for Edward oxenForde. Read the DNB article on Emmanuel Forde and marvel at his lack of any biographical footprint. The man is only a name. Geoffrey Bullough cites *Parismus* as a possible or likely "source" for *Twelfth Night*. *Parismus* contains an opening poem that could easily be from Oxford's youthful portfolio.

*The Famous Victories of Henry the Fifth*, 1598. This Anonymous proto-Henry the Fifth play was registered in 1594 with the other anonymous Ox-Shake plays (see above) but the 1598 quarto is the earliest surviving edition. This is another hotly debated play that has deep connections to the Earl of Oxford.

*Richard the Third* , Q2, 1598. "By    William    Shake-speare", Thomas Creede for Andrew Wise.

*Romeo and Juliet* , 1599, Anonymous. This is the Q2, but is the first "Good" or complete Quarto version of the play attributed by others to "Shakespeare". As described above, the procurement of the true text of *R&J* argues that Creede had access to real sources, and was not merely relying on actors remembrances or prompt books.

*The Wisdome of Doctor Dodypoll*, "As it hath bene sundry times acted by the Children of Paules.", 1600. There is no space to explain here, but I have argued, and other leading Oxfordian researchers agree, that *Dr. Dodypoll* is a very funny Oxford comedy that belongs in the Shake-speare Canon.

*The Weakest Goeth to the Wall*, 1600, "As it hath bene sundry times played by the right honorable Earle of Oxenford, Lord great Chamberlaine of England his servants." Anonymous. This quarto, like all the others on this list, features the Wounded Truth emblem.

The play is Anonymous. This is a key item of evidence because it clearly states on the Title Page that this is a play from Oxford's company's repertoire. The coincident registration and publication of *Weakest* with the play *The Wisdome of Dr. Dodypoll* suggests they came from the same source. Unfortunately, *Weakest* is a weak play by strict standards, and I'm not advocating it as emerging from the mature Oxford's pen. There is a lost play attributed to Munday that bears the same title. It is possible that this is the same play. One possibility is that *Weakest* is something that Oxford wrote in the 1570's and desired to see in print in 1600. Some of Oxford's friends (and enemies) were "gone to the wall" in 1600 and this may have prompted the printing. There also may be topical allusions that I haven't noticed yet. There is virtually no scholarship on the content of *Weakest*, only minor discussions about its curious existence.

Although Oxford's name appears as a dedicatee in the very earliest of Creede's printed quartos (*Card of Fancy*), this is the first, and I believe, the only instance in which Oxford's name ever appears anywhere **overtly** on the title page of a printed play. A third play from this batch that were registered together was called *The History of George Scanderberg*. It is credited in the Stationers' Register as an Oxford Company play, but all copies are lost, so we don't know what the printed work looked like or how good the play was.

*The Chronicle History of Henry the Fifth*, 1600. Anonymous. This is the Q1 and so-called "bad" quarto of "Shake-speare's" Henry the Fifth.

*Merrie wives of Windsor...*" by William Shakespeare", 1602. This is the "bad first quarto" of *Merry Wives*. The interesting thing is that Creede does NOT use the "Truth" emblem on this quarto

*Richard the Third*, Q3, 1602. "Newly augmented", "By William Shake-speare." Creede for A. Wise

*The London Prodigall*, 1605. The author credit is "by VVilliam Shakespeare". This is an Apocryphal play, and is so bad nobody wants to call it authentic. Perhaps Creede got desperate in 1605 with his prime source dead, and nothing new to print.

Thomas Creede's links to the Earl of Oxford dovetail with his ability to obtain true texts of Shakespeare, manuscripts of "Shakespeare Apocrypha", and works cited by historians as the sources that Shakespeare must have used.

# THE
## First part of the Tra-
gicall raigne of Selimus, sometime Empe-
rour of the Turkes, and grandfather to him
that now raigneth.

Wherein is showne how hee most vnnaturally
raised warres against his owne father Baiazet, and pre-
uailing therein, in the end caused him to
be poysoned:

Also with the murthering of his two brethren,
Corcut, and Acomat.

As it was playd by the Queenes Maiesties
Players.

LONDON
Printed by Thomas Creede, dwelling in Thames
streete at the signe of the Kathren wheele,
neare the olde Swanne.
1594

---

## COLIN CLOVTS
# Come home againe.

By Ed. Spencer.

LONDON
Printed for William Penfonbie.
1595.

---

# MENAECMI.
## ¶ A pleasant and fine Con-
ceited Comædie, taken out of the most excellent wittie Poet Plautus:

Chosen purposely from out the rest, as least harmefull, and
yet most delightfull.

Written in English, by W. W.

LONDON
Printed by Tho. Creede,
and are to be sold by William Barley, at his
shop in Gratious streete.
1595.

---

# THE
## True Tragedie of Ri-
chard the third:

Wherein is showne the death of Edward the
fourth, with the smothering of the two
yoong Princes in the Tower:

With a lamentable ende of Shores wife, an example
for all wicked women.

And lastly, the coniunction and ioyning of the two noble
Houses, Lancaster and Yorke.

As it was playd by the Queenes Maiesties
Players.

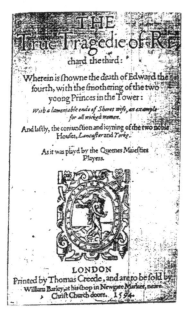

LONDON
Printed by Thomas Creede, and are to be sold by
William Barley, at his shop in Newgate Market, neare
Christ Church doore. 1594.

# GREENS,

## Groats-vvorth of VVit,

bought with a Million of
*Repentance.*

Describing the follie of youth, the falshoode of makeshift
flatterers, the miserie of the negligent, and mischiefes
of deceiuing Courtezans.

*VVritten before he before his death, and published at his
dying request.*

*Fælicem fuiße infaustum.*

### LONDON,

Printed by Thomas Creede, for Richard Oliue,
dwelling in long long Lane, and are there
to be solde. 1596.

---

# THE
## Mirror of Alchimy,

Composed by the thrice-famous and learned
Fryer, *Roger Bachon*, sometimes fellow of
*Martin* Colledge: and afterwards of
*Brasen-nose* Colledge in
*Oxenforde.*

Also a most excellent and learned discourse of
the admirable force and effacacie of Art and Nature,
written by the same *Author.*

With certaine other worthie Treatises of
the like Argument.

*Vino vendibili non opus est hedera.*

### LONDON
Printed for Richard Oliue.
1597.

---

Parismus,
# THE RENOV-
## MED PRINCE
### of Bohemia.

His most famous, delectable, and pleasant
*Historie.*

Containing

His Noble Battailes fought against the *Persians*, His
loue to *Laurana*, the Kings-Daughter of *Thessaly*:
And his strange Aduentures in the
*Desolate Iland.*

With the miseries and miserable imprisonments, *Laurana* endured in the Iland of *Rockes*, And a description of the
Chivalrie of the *Phrygian* Knight, *Pollipus*: and
his constant loue to *Violetta.*

*Dum spiro spero.*

Imprinted at London by Thomas Creede,
for Richard Oliue. 1598.

---

# THE
# FAMOVS VIC-
## tories of Henry the
### fifth:

## Containing the Honou-
rable Battell of Agin-court:

*As it was plaide by the Queenes Maiesties
Players.*

### LONDON
Printed by Thomas Creede, 1598.

# THE
# VVEAKEST
### goeth to the VVall.

*As it hath bene sundry times plaide by the right ho-
nourable Earle of Oxenford, Lord great
Chamberlaine of England
his seruants.*

## LONDON

Printed by Thomas Creede, for Richard
Oliue, dwelling in Long Lane.
1600.

---

# THE
# CRONICLE
### History of Henry the fift,
With his battell fought at *Agin Court* in
*France.* Togither with *Auntient*
*Pistoll.*

*As it hath bene sundry times ployd by the Right honorable
the Lord Chamberlaine his seruants.*

## LONDON

Printed by *Thomas Creede*, for Tho. Millington, and Iohn Busby. And are to be
sold at his house in Carter Lane, next
the Powle head. 1600.

---

# THE
### VVisdome of Doc-
### tor Dodypoll.

*As it hath bene sundrie times Acted
by the Children of Powles.*

## LONDON
Printed by Thomas Creede, for Richard
Oliue, dwelling in Long Lane.
1600.

---

# THE
# TRAGEDIE
### of King Richard
### the third.

*Conteining his treacherous Plotts against his brother
Clarence: the pittifull murther of his innocent Nephewes: his tyrannicall vsurpation: with the
whole course of his detested life, and
most deserued death,*

*As it hath bene lately Acted by the Right Honourable
the Lord Chamberlaine his seruants.*

Newly augmented,

By *William Shakespeare.*

## LONDON
Printed by Thomas Creede, for Andrew Wise, dwelling
in Paules Church-yard, at the signe of the
Angell. 1602.

# Chapter Sixteen

## Monsieur D'Olive

In 1606 Thomas Creede printed, for William Holmes, the first quarto of George Chapman's play Monsieur D'Olive. The title reads:

> Monsieur D'Olive. A comedie, as it was sundrie times acted by her Majesties children at the Blacke-Friers.

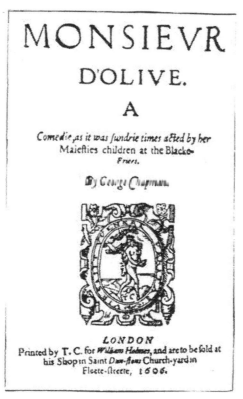

*Monsieur D'Olive* **title page.**

The quarto uses Creede's familiar Wounded Truth emblem. The drama inside tells a remarkable tale about an eccentric and flamboyant aristocrat who supports literature and the Arts. The portions of the play that feature the character

Monsieur D'Olive seem to tell the private side of Oxford's story. It is not out of the question that Chapman would write a memorial for Edward de Vere.

**George Chapman**, (c. 1559-1634) was a classical scholar, translator, dramatist and poet. He is linked at least three ways to the Vere family through his writings.

1. There is the famous flattering passage about the Earl of Oxford in Chapman's *The Revenge of Bussy D'Ambois*, a play printed in 1613, but thought to have been written as early as 1607.

Clermont:  "I over-took, coming from Italy, in Germany, a great and famous Earl of England; the most goodly fashioned man I ever saw: from head to foot in form rare, and most absolute; he had a face like one of the most ancient honored Romans, from whence his noblest Family was derived; He was beside of spirit passing great, **valiant, and learned, and liberal as the Sun, spoke and writ sweetly, or of learned subjects, or of the discipline of public weals; and t'was the Earl of Oxford**; and being offered at that time, by Duke Casimere, the view of his right royal Army then in field; refused it, and no foot was moved, to stir out his own free fore-determined course:
I wondering at it asked for his reason, it being an offer so much for his honor.
He, all acknowledging, said **t'was not fit,
To take those honors that one cannot quit**.
*Revenge of Bussy D'Ambois,* Act III, Scene 4

2. Chapman was friends with Oxford's daughter Susan de Vere the Countess Montgomery, the wife of the eventual patron of the Shakespeare *First Folio*. Chapman wrote a dedication poem to Susan that was published in his translation of the *Illiad*, in 1609.

To the Great and Vertuous, the Countess of Montgomerie:

Your Fame (great Lady) is so loud resounded,
By your free Trumpet, my right worthy friend;
That, with it, all my forces stand confounded,
Armed and disarmed at once, to one just end;
To honor and describe the blessed consent

Twixt your high blood and soul, in virtues rare.
Of which, my friends praise is so eminent,
That I shall hardly like his echo fair,
To render only the ends of his shrill Verse.
Besides; my bounds are short; and I must merely,
My will to honor your rare parts, rehearse;
With more time singing your renown more clearly
Mean-time, take Homer for my wants supply:
To whom adjoined your Name shall never die.

Oxford wrote a poem that uses an echo effect, and that lyric is what Chapman is alluding to here.

3. Chapman wrote a long poem in 1622 dedicated to and featuring the exploits of Horatio Vere, Oxford's cousin, who had recently died. The work is called *Pro Vere, Autumni Lachrymae. Inscribed to the Immortal Memory of the most Pious and Incomparable Soldier, Sir Horatio Vere, Knight.*

The quarto was printed by B. Alsop for Thomas Walkley in 1622. Isn't it interesting that in the same year that Walkley obtained a manuscript of *Othello* and printed it, he was working on Chapman's memorial to Oxford's trusted cousin Horatio. Perhaps Horatio's death freed up a boxed typescript.

Given Chapman's strong connections to the Vere family, the content of the play *Monsieur D'Olive,* and the language that the D'Olive speaks, there are strong reasons to identify the character Monsieur D'Olive with Oxford. He has the clichés and mannerisms that mark Oxford's style. Additionally, he mentions the mythical King Gyges and Gyges' ring, a rare allusion which appears in an Oxford poem. And there is the obvious symbol of the Olive which is green (ver) and is sacred to Minerva.

D'Olive :    Faith, sir, I had a poor roof or a penthouse to shade me
             from the sun, and three or four tiles to shroud me from
             the rain, and thought myself as private as I had King
             Gyges' ring, and could have gone invisible; yet saw all ...
             ... our great men
             Like to a mass of clouds and now seem like
             An elephant, and straightways like an ox

229

> And then a mouse: or like those changeable creatures
> that live in the burdello ...

D'Olive:    Well, well, let's leave these wit skirmishes, and say when shall we meet ?

Mugeron:    How think you, are we not met now?

D'Olive:    **Tush, man! I mean at my chamber, where we may take free use of ourselves; that is, drink sack, and talk satire, and let our wits run wild goose chase over court and country. I will have my chamber the rendezvous of all good wits, the shop of good words, the mint of good jests, an ordinary of fine discourse; critics, essayists, linguists, poets, and other professors of that faculty of wit, shall at certain hours i' th' day resort thither; it shall be a second Sorbonne ...**

This, I believe, is Chapman's recollection of Oxford's speaking style, from personal experience.

The next excerpt brings us almost into smoking-gun territory where the Olive/Oxford persona merges with a blend of Shakespeare references.

Duke :    But pray thee briefly say what said the weaver.

D'Olive:    The weaver, sir, much like the virginal Jack,
Start nimbly up; the colour of his beard
I scarce remember; but purblind he was
With the Geneva print, and wore one ear
Shorter than the other for a difference

> How oft when thou, my music, music play'st,
> Upon that blessed wood whose motion sounds
> With thy sweet fingers when thou gently sway'st
> The wiry concord that mine ear confounds,
> **Do I envy those jacks that nimble leap**,
> To kiss the tender inward of thy hand,
> Whilst my poor lips which should that harvest reap
> At the wood's boldness by thee blushing stand.
>     Sonnet 128

Oph.  There's rue for you, and here's some for me.
We may call it herb of grace o' Sundays.
**O, you must wear your rue with a difference!**
*Hamlet* Act IV Scene 5

# Selected Bibliography

| | |
|---|---|
| Arber, Edward | Transcript of the Registers of the Company of the Stationers of London, London & Birmingham: 1875-94 |
| Arber, Edward | An Introductory Sketch to the Martin Marprelate Controversy, Edinburgh: 1904 |
| Bennett, H. S. | English Books & Readers 1558 to 1603. Cambridge University Press: 1965 |
| Bullough, Geoffrey | Narrative and dramatic sources of Shakespeare (in 8 volumes), New York, Columbia University Press, 1957-75 |
| Burn, John S. | The Star Chamber. Notices of the Court & it's proceedings, London, 1870 |
| Chambers, E. K. | The Elizabethan Stage in 4 volumes. Oxford: Clarendon Press: 1974 |
| Chambers, E. K. | William Shakespeare: A study of facts and problems. Oxford: 1930 |
| Clark, Eva Turner. | Hidden Allusions in Shakespeare's Plays. New York: 1931 |
| Dennys, Rodney | The Heraldic Imagination. New York: 1975 |
| Duff, E.G. | A Century of the English Book Trade. London: 1905 |
| Fowler, William P. | Shakespeare Revealed in Oxford's Letters. Portsmouth, N. H.: 1986 |
| Gillett, Charles R. | Burned Books - Neglected Chapters in British History & Literature. Columbia Univ. Press, New York: 1932 |
| Greg, W. W. | The decrees and Ordinances of the Stationers' Company. London: 1928 |
| Greg, W. W. | Dramatic Documents from the Elizabethan Playhouses. Oxford: 1931 |
| Greg, W. W. | Henslowe's diary. London: 1904 |
| Greg, W. W. | Records of the Court of the Stationers Co. 1576-1602. London: 1930 |
| Hazlitt, W.C. | The livery Companies of the City of London. London: 1892 |
| Judge, Cyril B. | Elizabethan Book Pirates. Harvard Univ. Press, Cambridge. 1934 |
| Kirschbaum, Leo | Shakespeare and the Stationers. Columbus: Ohio U. Press: 1955 |
| Lee, Sir Sidney | A life of William Shakespeare. New York: 1909 |
| McKerrow, R. B. | A Dictionary of Printers and Booksellers in England, Scotland, and Ireland ... 1557-1640. Bibliographical Society, London: 1910 |
| McKerrow, R. B. | Printers and Publishers' devices in England, Scotland, and Ireland ... 1485-1640. Bibliographical Society, |

London: 1913

McKerrow, R.B.     The Works of Thomas Nashe. 5 volumes. Oxford: 1958

Miller, Ruth Lloyd     Shakespeare Identified / Oxfordian Vistas Volumes 1 & 2. Kennikat Press, Port Washington, NY: 1975

Ogburn, Charlton     The Mysterious William Shakespeare: The Myth and the Reality. New York: 1984

Ogburn, Sr., C. & D.     This Star of England. New York: 1952

Pollard, A. W.     Shakespeare Folios and Quartos. London, 1909

Pollard, A. W.     Shakespeare's Fight with the Pirates. Cambridge University Press, 1920

Pollard, Alfred W. F.     A Short title catalogue of books printed in England, Scotland and Ireland and of English books printed abroad, 1475-1640. Shakespeare Birthplace Trust. Library: 1955

Plomer, H. R.     Abstracts of Wills of English Printers 1492-1630. Bibliographical Society, London: 1903

Smith, Irwin.     Shakespeare's Blackfriars Playhouse Its History and its design. NYU Press, New York: 1964

Williams, Franklin.     Index of Dedications and Commendatory Verses in English Books before 1641. Bibliographical Society, London: 1962

13917290R00140